The Highlights at a Glance

The numbers on the red dots refer to page numbers in the book.

Clemens Beeck
Günter Schneider (Photos)

Berlin
Highlights

The Practical Guide for
Discovering the City

Jaron Verlag

This book is available in the following languages:
German/English/French/Italian/Spanish/Russian

Illustrations
Front Cover: Brandenburg Gate
Page 2: The Reichstag Building's cupola
Page 6 Europacenter with the Memorial Church
Page 127: Neptune Fountain in front of the Television Tower
Back cover (from top left): Reichstag Building, towers at Potsdamer Platz, Bismarck Monument and Victory Column at Grosser Stern, World Clock at Alexanderplatz, New National Gallery, German Historical Museum

Extended and updated edition
2nd Printing of this edition 2016

(Original title: "Highlights in Berlin. Der praktische Begleiter für Entdeckungstouren durch die Stadt")

www.jaron-verlag.de
Translation: Miriamne Fields, Berlin
Map (Page 1): Matthias Frach, Berlin
Public transporation map (Page 128): Berliner Verkehrsbetriebe
Cover design: Bauer+Möhring, Berlin, using photographs by Günter Schneider
Typography: Prill partners | producing, Berlin/Barcelona
Repro: Bild1Druck GmbH, Berlin
Printed and bound by: Westermann Druck Zwickau GmbH, Zwickau

ISBN 978-3-89773-684-9
ISBN 978-3-89773-685-6 (5 copies)

Berlin Highlights from Alex to the Zoo

No capital in Europe is as "young" as Berlin. A quarter of a century since the city's division ended, this megalopolis appears confident and colorful with a newly designed center. This once slumbering city enclosed by a wall has turned into a vibrant metropolis that has never enjoyed greater popularity. Onlookers from all over the world are drawn to the Spree.

Visitors to Berlin won't be disappointed. The dynamic with which the German capital is changing is impressive. It is courageously facing modernity without relinquishing its identity. And Berlin has the reputation throughout the world of being a liberal and open city.

It is by now difficult to keep track of all the attractions in the city. They span from the courtly historic architecture on Unter den Linden to spectacular new buildings such as the Jewish Museum and the Federal Chancellery in the new Government Quarter; from the many art treasures found on the Museum Island – one of the most unique museum ensembles in the world – to the many-facetted Cultural Forum with its glistening modern temples; from the hip and trendy Mitte and Prenzlauer Berg districts to the bustling City-West; from the lively shopping mile along Friedrichstrasse to the quiet hidden-away back courtyards.

To make your visit to Berlin a varied and relaxing experience, this special kind of city guide provides quick and informative explanations to help you find the highlights in the German capital. Short texts provide you with everything you need to know about each site and the numerous photos give you an excellent impression of the special charm of the metropolis on the Spree. Addresses, opening hours, directions, a practical information section, a city map, a public transportation map and two registers make it easy for you to plan the details of your journey through Berlin.

BZ
fitness first

This book reveals the exciting mix of old and new that makes Berlin what it is today. The new city districts such as Potsdamer Platz are just as typical of the city as are the many vestiges of its rich past. Berlin has many sites that reveal Germany's changing history. Take for example the Brandenburg Gate, a former city gate which became a symbol of German unity. Or the unusual architecture from the period of Frederick the Great, which reflects Prussia's dedication to scholarship and culture. There are also many lovely palaces in both Berlin and its neighbor, Potsdam – the Prussian residence city where Frederick the Great began the creation of a world masterpiece: the Sanssouci Palace and Park.

Traces of the 40 year long division can also be found in the city. The remains of the Berlin Wall, for example, exist in various forms: as an admonishing memorial, as a colorful canvas of artistic fantasies and yearnings, and as a reconstructed border patrol at Checkpoint Charlie. These reminders of a sad chapter in history become all the more important as more people grow up without any personal memory of the divided city.

But Berlin is also a Mecca for people in search of nightlife and entertainment. Decked out starlets and tireless strollers flow into the many bars and outdoor cafes. They meet in the popular hangouts of Prenzlauer Berg, Kreuzberg and Mitte, for instance at Hackescher Markt – the place for nightlife in Berlin. Or they visit what are by now established niches of the alternative scene, such as the Kulturbrauerei. But if you are in need of quiet and relaxation, you can seek out a picturesque location like the Peacock Island or visit the Tiergarten park, an oasis in the middle of the city.

Variety and diversity are the trademarks of Berlin. We have made this book to ensure that you don't miss any of the attractive, famous and exciting places in Berlin. Let it help you to discover one of the most interesting cities in the world.

Alexanderplatz
Alexanderplatz

Alexanderplatz is a central traffic junction and therefore densely populated. The unusual **World Clock**, built in 1969, is a popular place for people to meet. The site even achieved literary fame: In his novel "Berlin Alexanderplatz" (1929), Alfred Döblin immortalized the plaza as a place for ordinary people. Despite its alluring name, its appearance is rather paltry. After the war and post-war reconstruction the plaza resembled little more than a barren concrete wasteland. When Alexanderplatz was built into the center area of the "GDR capital" in 1966–72 and the → **Television Tower** was erected on the edge of the plaza, it lost its human proportions entirely. But over time this totalitarian setting has reverted back into a pleasant urban area. The **Galeria Kaufhof** is quite worthwhile. It was once the "Centrum Warenhaus," the largest department store in all of East Germany. The architect Josef Paul Kleihues remodeled it in 2004–06, adding Berlin's most impressive atrium. Many people enjoy taking a break at the **Friendship Among Nations Fountain** (1969) in front of the store's entrance.
Alexa, Berlin's largest shopping center on Alexanderstrasse, also has a spacious design. The imaginatively decorated shopping mall bears stylistic references to art deco elements. The oldest buildings on the plaza, the **Alexanderhaus** and **Berolinahaus**, built by Peter Behrens in 1929–32, are examples of early modernism.

▷ S- and U-Bahn station Alexanderplatz

Eastern center of the city: Alexanderplatz with hotel tower

Showing the earth's time zones for almost a half century: the World Clock

One of the most attractive shopping centers in Berlin: Alexa

An old department store in a new look: Galeria Kaufhof with the Friendship Among Nations Fountain

(Clockwise from top left)

Berliner Dom
Berlin Cathedral

The Berlin Cathedral, the largest Protestant church in Germany, is a must for church-lovers. Built in 1894–1905 at the edge of the → **Museum Island** according to plans by Julius Raschdorff, it served both as the main Prussian Protestant church and as the court church of the ruling Hohenzollerns. The richly decorated building of Silesian granite – with the dome cross – once stood 114 meters high. Severely damaged during the war, it was later more modestly rebuilt. The dome roof was designed more simply, the main dome with the cross is now only 98 meters high. The memorial church on the north side was torn down.
Rededicated on June 6, 1993, the cathedral's interior is surprising in its magnificence and rather typical of a Catholic church. Visitors can also enter the Hohenzollern crypt, where almost 100 coffins have been preserved. A few resplendent sarcophagi – including those of the Great Elector and Electress Dorothea – are on display inside the church.
The **Lustgarten** in front of the cathedral has changed form many times over its four-century-long history. The current design dates back to plans by Karl Friedrich Schinkel from 1828–32, while the fountain is contemporary. The landscaped plaza was once a part of the **Berlin City Palace**, whose façade is being reconstructed across from the cathedral.

Am Lustgarten
Mon–Sat 9am–8pm, Sun 12pm–8pm
Tel. 20 26 91 64; www.berlinerdom.de

▷ S-Bahn station Hackescher Markt, bus 100, 200

Prussia's glory: the Berlin Cathedral with Schinkel's palace bridge

Wilhelminian grandeur: the elaborately restored church hall

Viewed from the cathedral dome: the Lustgarten

A welcoming cool-down in summer: the Lustgarten fountains

(Clockwise from top)

Brandenburger Tor
Brandenburg Gate

The Brandenburg Gate, Berlin's most famous landmark, is over 220 years old. Until 1989 it symbolized the division of Berlin and Germany; today it is a national symbol of unity. The structure is the only remaining city gate in Berlin. Its leads out of the historic city center into the → **Tiergarten**. Carl Gotthard Langhans modeled it after the Propylaeum in Athens in 1789–91, making it the first significant example of antique classicism in Berlin. Later this architectural style became so influential that the city acquired the nick-name "Athens on the Spree." Originally, the façade of Elbe sandstone was painted white. Johann Gottfried Schadow, who created the façade ornamentation, also designed the "Quadriga," the four-horsed chariot at the top. After Prussia and its allies defeated Napoleon in 1814, the iron cross, designed by Karl Friedrich Schinkel, was added to the goddess of peace on the two-wheeled chariot, turning her into the goddess of victory. The Brandenburg Gate was severely damaged in World War II and the Quadriga completely destroyed. In 1956 the structure was restored and in 1958 the Quadriga, remade from a preserved cast, was again displayed.
After construction on the Berlin Wall began on August 13, 1961, the Brandenburg Gate at → **Pariser Platz** was off-limits to "normal mortals." It stood alone and isolated in the no-man's land of the East German border. Finally, on December 22, 1989, amid great media fanfare, a hole was broken through the Wall at the gate, and East and West were joined again.

▷ S- and U-Bahn station Brandenburger Tor

She crowns the most famous Berlin gate: the Quadriga with the goddess Victoria

Symbol of German unity: the Brandenburg Gate

Old warriors: world history re-enacted in front of the world famous landmark

Built in 1789–91 as the western city gate: a masterpiece of Classicism

(Clockwise from top left)

Checkpoint Charlie
Checkpoint Charlie

A quarter of a century after the Berlin Wall fell on November 9, 1989, the former border crossing at Checkpoint Charlie on → **Friedrichstrasse** has become one of the most important sites commemorating the division of Berlin. The checkpoint that had existed between the American (Kreuzberg) and Soviet (Mitte) sectors was a focal point of the cold war. After the Wall was built on August 13, 1961, the conflict escalated to the threat of war in October 1961, when combat-ready tanks of both super powers stood in a face-off here. Today a wooden barrack with sand sacks – a 2001 replica of a U.S. Army post – recalls this tense moment in history. The white sign with the warning "You are leaving the American sector" is, however, an original. The history of this site and of the Berlin Wall is presented on large outdoor exhibit panels. Cobblestones imbedded in the pavement mark the line of the border. The private commercially-run **House at Checkpoint Charlie** documents the subject of division and escape in detail. Two blocks from Checkpoint Charlie, when heading east on Zimmerstrasse, a column commemorates Peter Fechter, an 18-year-old who was fatally wounded by East German border guards when he tried to escape in 1962.

House at Checkpoint Charlie
Friedrichstrasse 43–45
Open daily 9am–10pm
Tel. 253 72 50; www.mauermuseum.de

▷ U-Bahn station Kochstrasse

Popular among tourists from all over the world: the museum at the historic border crossing

Documenting the division of Berlin: House at Checkpoint Charlie

Focal point of the cold war: replica of the US Army guardhouse

Outdoor exhibition: all about the fateful years of East-West division

(Clockwise from top left)

AUS AM CHECKPOINT CHARLIE
MAUERSHOP IM M

1961
PANZER-KONFRONTATION
TANK CONFRONTATION

US ARMY CHECKPOINT
YOU ARE LEAVING
THE AMERICAN SECTOR

Dorotheenstädtischer Friedhof
Dorotheenstadt Cemetery

Every big city has a cemetery for its famous daughters and sons. In Berlin the tombstones in the Dorotheenstadt Cemetery at Chausseestrasse read like a "Who's Who" of Germany's intellectual elite.

The cemetery was established in 1762 and continued to be enlarged until 1826. The famous people buried there include the philosophers Georg Wilhelm Friedrich Hegel and Johann Gottlieb Fichte; the authors Heinrich Mann, Bertolt Brecht, Johannes R. Becher, Arnold Zweig, Anna Seghers, and Christa Wolf; the playwright Heiner Müller; the architects Friedrich August Stüler and Karl Friedrich Schinkel; the artist John Heartfield; the actress Helene Weigel; and the book printer Ernst Theodor Litfass. It is also the final resting place of Federal President Johannes Rau.

There are also countless creative sculptural works to admire during a walk through the cemetery. The oldest classicist gravestone dates back to 1807 and was made for the manufacturer Jacob Fröhlich. The bust of the industrialist August Borsig was created by Christian Daniel Rauch.

The **Brecht House** is located at the entrance to the cemetery.

Chausseestrasse 126
Open daily 8am until dusk

Brecht Weigel Memorial
Chausseestrasse 125
Viewing only with a tour
Tel. 200 57 18 44; www.adk.de

▷ U-Bahn station Oranienburger Tor

Impressive: gravesite of the Hoffmann family of industrialists

Simple: sepulchral stele for the playwright Heiner Müller

Artistic: gravestone for the famous master builder Karl Friedrich Schinkel

At home right next to the cemetery: the artist-couple Brecht-Weigel

(Clockwise from top)

Bertolt Brecht

CARL FRIEDRICH SCHINKEL
GEBOREN
AM XIII MÄRZ MDCCLXXXI
GESTORBEN
AM IX OCTOBER MDCCCXLI

Heiner
Müller

East Side Gallery
East Side Gallery

The East Side Gallery is the longest monument for peace and reconciliation in Berlin. In 1990, with division over, artists from all over the world painted 1.3 kilometers of the dismal East German border wall along Mühlenstrasse. The colorful collection of political and poetic murals is a unique attraction.
Unfortunately automobile exhaust fumes and willful vandalism have taken their toll on the East Side Gallery. Some of the artists whose works were no longer recognizable painted their pictures again in 2009, returning them to their former glory.
The spontaneous work of art between → **Oberbaum Bridge** and Ostbahnhof has meanwhile been placed under historical preservation. It gives testimony to the hopes and effusive joy that was felt in Berlin after the Wall fell. It is an irony that the only preserved paintings on the Berlin Wall are located on former GDR territory: When the city was still divided, only the west side of the concrete wall could be painted. A small section of the once continuous East Side Gallery was interrupted to allow access to the bank of the Spree.
Arena am Ostbahnhof, Berlin's largest multipurpose stadium, stands right across the street.

A dream comes true: into the West with the Trabbi car

Meters of artwork: East Side Gallery on Mühlenstrasse

Restored in 2009: Artistically designed hope for peace

Berlin's largest event stadium: the Arena am Ostbahnhof

Art for sale: souvenir shop at the wall gallery

(Clockwise from top left)

Mühlenstrasse between Oberbaum Bridge and Ostbahnhof

▷ S-Bahn station Ostbahnhof, S- and U-Bahn station Warschauer Strasse

POLITIK IST DIE FORTSETZUNG DES KRIEGES
MIT ANDEREN MITTELN.
Tolerance
www.marymackeyart.com
USA

MEIN GOTT HILF MIR DIESE TÖDLICHE LIEBE ZU ÜBERLEBEN
STORE AT THE
EAST-SIDE GALLERY
ALLIED
CHECKPOINT
CHARLIE
Eingang
Entrance
Pass-
kontrolle
SOUVENIRS
CAF 1991

amnesty international

Mercedes-Benz Arena

Fernsehturm
Television Tower

It is common for large cities to have a broadcasting tower. That this technical and modest structure is situated in the center of the city is a peculiarity of Berlin. The Television Tower on the west side of → **Alexanderplatz** is 368 meters high and is the tallest structure in Berlin, conspicuously marking the center of the capital.

The idea for the massive structure came from the architects Henselmann and Streitparth. The old-town quarter between **Schlossplatz** and Alexanderplatz lay in ruins after the war. The East German government wanted to replace the clustered area that was now located in communist East Berlin with a modern center. The tower, built in 1965–69, was known as "Ulbricht's show-off piece" and hinted at the communist leaders' political and economic claim to leadership. The structure remains one of Europe's highest towers.

Visitors from all over the world enjoy the panoramic view from the visitors' platform and restaurant in the seven story globe. It stands 203 meters above ground and rotates around its own axis.

Panoramastrasse 1a
March–Oct. 9am to midn.; Nov.–Feb. 10am to midn.
Tel. 247 57 58 75; www.tv-turm.de

▷ S- and U-Bahn station Alexanderplatz

A Berlin landmark: the Television Tower

It revolves around its own axis twice every hour: tower globe with restaurant

Between the Cathedral, Town Hall and Alexanderplatz station: the city's highest structure

(Clockwise from top)

Friedrichstrasse
Friedrichstrasse

The north-south axis in the center of Berlin underwent an extraordinary revival after the Wall fell in 1989. Countless building projects led to the emergence of a completely new shopping mile between → **Checkpoint Charlie** and the **Friedrichstrasse Station**.
Its centerpieces are the **Friedrichstadt-Passagen** with the French department store **Galeries Lafayette** (at the corner of Französische Strasse), designed by Jean Nouvel; the **Quartier 206** with exclusive posh boutiques, built by Henry N. Cobb; and the **Quartier 205** by Oswald Mathias Ungers. Friedrichstrasse had once been an entertainment strip, both notorious and legendary. Today the tradition of variety stages and glamorous revue theaters is kept alive in the **Admiralspalast** and **Friedrichstadtpalast**, just north of the train station. The **Berliner Ensemble** at Schiffbauerdamm, once the workplace of the famous playwright Bertolt Brecht (1898–1956), is one of Germany's most influential theaters. When Berlin was still a divided city, the Friedrichstrasse Station from 1882 had a sad role to play. Today an exhibition inside the glass pavilion known as **Tränenpalast** (Palace of Tears) recalls that between 1963 and 1990 the lively traffic junction here served as an official checkpoint between East and West Berlin.

Galeries Lafayette
Friedrichstrasse 76–78
www.galerieslafayette.de

▷ U-Bahn station Stadtmitte

Tränenpalast
Reichstagufer 17
Tue–Fri 9am–7pm, Sat/Sun 10am–6pm
Tel. 46 77 77 90; www.hdg.de

▷ S and U-Bahn station Friedrichstrasse

Bright lights: the French department store Galeries Lafayette and Quartier 206

Entertainment palace with a hundred-year history: the Admiralspalast

Fashionably chic: elegant boutiques on Friedrichstrasse

Between the Spree and Friedrichstrasse station: modern office buildings behind the blue Palace of Tears

(Clockwise from top left)

Friedrichswerder
Friedrichswerder

One of the oldest sections of Berlin lies between → **Gendarmenmarkt** and → the **Museum Island**, just beyond the avenue → **Unter den Linden**. Founded in the 17th century and destroyed by war and totalitarian urban planning in the 20th century, the area of Friedrichswerder today is undergoing a renaissance.
Only the **Friedrichswerder Church**, built in 1824–30, survived the turmoil of history. The neo-gothic house of worship was designed by master builder Karl Friedrich Schinkel. Today it serves as a museum for classicist sculptures, showing works by the important Berlin sculptors Rauch and Schadow. It also provides information about the life and work of Schinkel. The influential architect is honored by **Schinkelplatz**, the attractive plaza bearing his name.
The **Foreign Office** stands across the street from the church. The federal ministry works in a huge complex, the older part of which was built in 1934–40 for the Reichsbank. For 30 years during the era of the GDR, this building was the headquarters of the all-powerful SED, the ruling party in East Germany.
The nearby **townhouses**, narrow residential homes of contemporary architecture, bring a picturesque old-town flair back to the area.
Until World War II, the peaceful **Hausvogteiplatz** was the capital's fashion district.
The **Jungfernbrücke** of 1798, Berlin's oldest drawbridge, is found on the Spree Canal along side the Foreign Office.

Friedrichswerder Church
Werderscher Markt
Open daily 10am–6pm
Tel. 266 42 42 42; www.smb.museum

▷ U-Bahn station Hausvogteiplatz

Modern architecture at Friedrichswerder: townhouses

Old and new side by side: the Friedrichswerder Church reflected in the Foreign Office

Idyllic setting on the Spree Canal: the Foreign Office

On display in the Schinkel church: works by Berlin sculptors

(Clockwise from top left)

Gärten der Welt
Gardens of the World

The Gardens of the World, a 21-hectare landscaped park with exotic and traditional garden art, is an unusual attraction on the east side of the city. Located within the **Marzahn Recreational Park**, it contains flourishing gardens with original building material and plants from different countries such as China, Japan and Korea.

The Chinese Garden is among the largest of its kind situated outside of China. The Japanese grounds, imbued with symbolism, were designed by a Zen priest. Specialists from Morocco created the Oriental Garden in the classical style of the Moors, who saw paradise reflected within the geometric oasis. Another highlight is the Renaissance Garden, which impressively depicts the beginnings of European landscape architecture. The Christian Garden brings a new interpretation to the traditional cloister colonnade: the square terrain is enclosed by airy gold-walls made of letters – biblical texts and philosophical pieces of wisdom.

Visitors can test their sense of direction in the labyrinth, which is made of 1250 yew trees.

Eisenacher Strasse 99
Open daily until dusk
Tel. 700 90 66 99; www.gaerten-der-welt.de

▷ S-Bahn station Marzahn, U-Bahn station Cottbusser Platz, then bus 195

Italy in Marzahn: the Renaissance Garden

Green maze: labyrinth in the recreational park

New interpretation of a cloister colonnade: the Christian Garden

Attractive setting on the lake: Chinese Garden

(Clockwise from top left)

Gedächtniskirche
Memorial Church

The **Breitscheidplatz**, the center of West-City and the start of the → **Kurfürstendamm**, is the most crowded plaza in all Berlin. For over 100 years the shopping district in Charlottenburg has been marked by the Emperor Wilhelm Memorial Church (Kaiser-Wilhelm-Gedächtniskirche).

Built in 1891–95 according to plans by Franz Schwechten, the sandstone house of worship once stood 113 meters high with an interior decorated with mosaics. After the vast destruction of World War II, the tower ruins were preserved as a monument against war. The torso is flanked on both sides by modern church structures built in 1957–61. The octagonal hall for prayer services and the six-sided bell tower were designed by Egon Eiermann. Gabriel Loire's glass painting set in concrete infuses the rooms in a deep blue light.

The 22-story **Europacenter** was erected in 1963–65 by Helmut Hentrich and Hubert Petschnigg but has been redesigned many times since then. It incorporates a shopping center. In front is the red granite **World Globe Fountain**. The **Bikini House** on Budapester Strasse, another child of the post-war era, is being entirely renovated.

Within view of the Memorial Church, a branch of the legendary New York **Waldorf-Astoria Hotel** opened in a highrise in 2012.

Emperor Wilhelm Memorial Church
Breitscheidplatz
Church: open daily 9am–7pm
Tower ruins: Mon–Sat 10am–4pm
www.gedaechtniskirche-berlin.de

▷ S- and U-Bahn station Zoologischer Garten

Across from the church: the new luxury hotel Waldorf-Astoria

Prayer services: modern church structure by Egon Eiermann

Striking Berlin landmark: the ruins of the Memorial Church

Between church and zoo: renovated Bikini-Haus behind the Zoo Palast

(Clockwise from top left)

Gedenkstätte Berliner Mauer
Berlin Wall Memorial

The Berlin Wall Memorial, located at Bernauer Strasse, commemorates the division of Berlin from 1961–89. The street once formed the border between the western and eastern sectors and was the site of many tragic escape attempts. People who lived on the sealed-off side in East Berlin jumped out of windows to reach freedom in the West. Today a detailed exhibition along the outdoor grounds where the inhuman barrier stood for 28 years provides information about these dramatic events.
Victims of the division are also commemorated on the expansive terrain that runs between Brunnenstrasse and Nordbahnhof. Corroded metal poles as high as the concrete wall that once stood there mark the former border, conveying an impression of the Berlin Wall's hermetic character.
A monument on Ackerstrasse contains a small preserved section of the original border fortifications. Another exhibition is shown inside the **Berlin Wall Museum and Documentation Center** located across street. From the center's viewing platform visitors get a good impression of the border that once cut through the entire city. The **Chapel of Reconciliation** stands nearby. It was erected to replace the original Church of Reconciliation that the East German government ordered to be torn down in 1985.
Tourists begin their visit at the **Visitor Center** at Nordbahnhof.

Berlin Wall Documentation and Visitor Center
Bernauer Strasse 111/119
Tue–Sun 9:30am–6pm, Apr.–Oct. until 7pm
Tel. 467 98 66 66;
www.berliner-mauer-gedenkstaette.de

▷ U-Bahn st. Bernauer Strasse, S-Bahn st. Nordbahnhof

Monument with watchtower at the former border: the Berlin Wall Memorial

On the grounds of the blown-up Reconciliation Church: the Chapel of Reconciliation from 1999

Next to the Wall remains: Visitor Center on Bernauer Strasse

(Clockwise from top)

LINER MAUER

Kapelle der Versöhnung

Gendarmenmarkt
Gendarmenmarkt

The Gendarmenmarkt is one of the loveliest plazas in Europe. The ensemble created by the Schauspielhaus (playhouse) and the two dome buildings at each side is quite singular. In 1780–85 Carl von Gontard added identical non-functional towers to the two previously unremarkable churches. The **German Church** was rebuilt more simply after it was damaged in the war and now houses an exhibition on the history of the German Parliament. In the **French Church** on the north side of the square a museum presents the history of the Huguenots and the role they played in Berlin. This religious minority that was persecuted in France was welcomed here with open arms beginning in 1685. Soon every fifth resident in the Spree city was speaking French.

The **Schauspielhaus** (used today as a concert hall) was built in 1818–21 and is one of the main works of the Prussian architect Karl Friedrich Schinkel (1781–1841). The Schiller Monument was set in front of the Schauspielhaus in 1871. On Charlottenstrasse, behind the Schinkel building, you'll find the traditional restaurant **Lutter & Wegner**. Two frequent guests to the more then 200-year-old wine tavern, the author E.T.A. Hoffmann and the actor Ludwig Devrient, coined the German word for sparkling wine: Sekt.

German Church
Gendarmenmarkt 1
Tue–Sun 10am–6pm, May–Sept. until 7pm
Tel. 22 73 04 31; www.bundestag.de

Huguenot Museum
Gendarmenmarkt 5
Tue–Sat 12pm–5pm, Sun 11am–5pm
Tel. 229 17 60; www.franzoesischer-dom.de

▷ U-Bahn station Stadtmitte

Used today as a concert hall: the Schauspielhaus by Schinkel

Showpiece in front of the German church: Schiller Monument by Reinhold Begas

The loveliest square in the capital: Gendarmenmarkt with the Schauspielhaus und churches from the time of Frederick the Great

(Clockwise from top left)

Hackescher Markt

Hackescher Markt

Hackescher Markt is one of Berlin's most popular sites. The gate to the old city quarter Spandauer Vorstadt magically allures passers-by and entertainment-seekers. The plaza is frequented well into the wee hours of the night.
Its main attraction is the **Hackesche Höfe**, a passageway of eight courtyards built in 1906 by the architect Kurt Berndt. The mix of gastronomy, cinema, clubs, variety shows, boutiques, bookstores, souvenir shops and apartments is one-of-a-kind. The first courtyard's art nouveau façade created by August Endell is well worth a look. The neighborhood contains a number of very attractive courtyards as well.
The back entrance of the Hackesche Höfe leads to **Sophienstrasse** with its picturesque architecture. The **Sophien Church** (entrance at Grosse Hamburger Strasse) contains the only preserved baroque church tower in all of Berlin (built in 1732–34). It is 69 meters high.
An example of the creative flair of the Spandauer Vorstadt is found at the **Sophie-Gips-Höfe**, courtyards artistically designed with light installations, garden art and painting by the patrons Erika and Rolf Hoffmann. **August-**

Hackesche Höfe
Rosenthaler Strasse 40/41
www.hackesche-hoefe.com

Sophie-Gips-Höfe
Sophienstrasse 21
Tel. 28 49 91 20; www.sammlung-hoffmann.de

Sophien Church
Grosse Hamburger Strasse 29
May–Sept. Wed 3pm–6pm, Sat until 5pm
www.sophien.de

▷ S-Bahn station Hackescher Markt, U-Bahn station Weinmeisterstrasse

Evidence of history on Sophienstrasse: portal of Berlin artisans

Highlight among the densely built old-town of Berlin: the Hackescher Markt

New building in the traditional style: New Hackescher Markt

Lovingly restored: Jugendstil façade in the Hackesche Höfe

(Clockwise from top left)

DIE HACKESCHEN HÖFE
oxymoron
Heinrich Böll Stiftung
Hanley's
kleiner festsaal
trippen
MÖBELRESTAURATOR
maz&movie
KUNSTBUCH
FILMTHEATER
HACKESCHES HOFTHEATER
AMPELMANN SHOP
PUMA
HACKESCHER HOF

TRATTORIA
CAFETERIA

In memory of the advertising pillar's inventor: the Litfass-Platz

Relic from the time of the emperor on Neue Schönhauser Strasse: the "Volkskaffeehaus"

Commotion in front of the venerable station: Hackescher Markt

Art in all it facets: gallery on Auguststrasse

(Clockwise from top left)

strasse is dominated by art rather than commerce and is home to a number of art galleries, including KunstWerke.
Berlin's very successful young international fashion world presents its creations mostly on Alte and Neue Schönhauser Strasse and on Münzstrasse.
The **S-Bahn station Hackescher Markt** is one of the oldest existing stations in Berlin and the loveliest one along the urban rail built in 1875–82. At **Litfass-Platz** on the other side of the attractive brick and terracotta railroad structure, you'll find interesting contemporary architecture (2010) with old-town dimensions.

Volks=Kaffee=u.Speise=Hallen Ges.

Hauptbahnhof
Main Station

The commanding cathedral-like structure of the Berlin Main Station is unique to Europe. Two rail lines intersect here on different levels. The east-west route runs four stories above the underground north-south axis. This bold construction was designed by the office von Gerkan, Marg & Partner, and has become a sight-seeing attraction since it opened in May 2006. Berlin's oldest preserved train station is located on Invalidenstrasse, close by. The **Hamburg Station** was built in 1846/47 and serves today as a Museum of Contemporary Art, showing works from the second half of the 20th century and exhibitions of contemporary artists. Its collection includes works by Joseph Beuys, Anselm Kiefer, the "Junge Wilde" and Andy Warhol. The light installation on the classical entrance façade was made by Dan Flavin. Another nearby highlight is the **Museum of Natural History**. The collection is over 200 years old and contains many fascinating artifacts in addition to the largest exhibited dinosaur skeleton worldwide. The "wet collection," with almost a million animal preparations displayed in glass cases, is also impressive.

Hamburg Station – Museum of Contemporary Art
Invalidenstrasse 50/51
Tue–Sun 10am–6pm, Thu until 8pm, Sat/Sun 11am–6pm
Tel. 266 42 42 42; www.smb.museum

▷ S- and U-Bahn station Hauptbahnhof

Museum of Natural History
Invalidenstrasse 43
Tue–Fri 9:30–6pm, Sat/Sun 10am–6pm
Tel. 20 93 85 91; www.naturkundemuseum-berlin.de

▷ U-Bahn station Naturkundemuseum

Modern cathedral: Berlin's main station

Berlin's newest station: intercity express train meets Berlin's commuter rail

Berlin's oldest train station building: the Hamburg Station as an art museum

Berlin's oldest skeleton: dinosaur in the Museum of Natural History

(Clockwise from top left)

Holocaust-Mahnmal
Holocaust Memorial

Berlin does not try to hide the fact that the city served as the headquarters of the National Socialist terror regime from 1933–45. The unfathomable atrocities committed by the Nazi dictatorship, in particular the horrible mass murder of six million Jews, is officially commemorated right in the center of the German capital, not far from → **Wilhelmstrasse**, which was once the power center of the Nazis. The "Memorial for the Murdered Jews of Europe", located south of the → **Brandenburg Gate**, was dedicated in 2005. Over 2000 visitors daily stride through the uneven and confusing narrow passageways formed by the 2711 concrete slabs of varying height.

The New York architect Peter Eisenman intended for his design of the Holocaust Memorial to instill in its visitors a feeling of insecurity and trepidation.

The Information Center, located in an underground area, provides historical information about the Shoah. In contrast to the abstract Field of Stelae, the "Room of Names" is dedicated to the individual fates of Holocaust victims. Their biographical dates are projected on the wall as their names are read over a loudspeaker.

The "Monument to Homosexuals Persecuted under National Socialism" is also nearby (Ebertstrasse, corner of Lennéstrasse).

Memorial for the Murdered Jews of Europe
Cora-Berliner-Strasse 1
Information Center: Apr.–Sept. Tue–Sun 10am–8pm, Oct.–March until 7pm
Tel. 263 94 30; www.holocaust-denkmal.de
▷ S- und U-Bahn station Brandenburger Tor

Underground: the Information Center

Bird's eye view: the Holocaust memorial's huge "field of stelae"

With Potsdamer Platz architecture as backdrop: 2711 stones commemorating the murdered Jews of Europe

Individual fates of Nazi victims: exhibition on the Shoah

(Clockwise from top left)

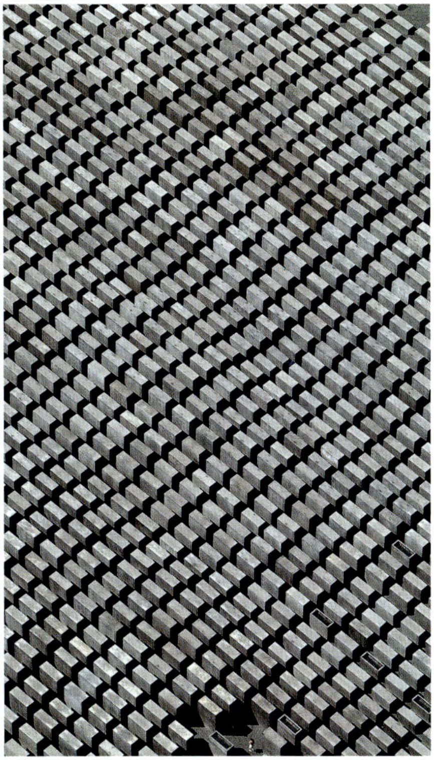

Jüdisches Museum
Jewish Museum

The unique and expressive architecture designed by Daniel Libeskind is one reason why the Berlin Jewish Museum is a must-see for visitors from all over the world. The famous American architect wanted to make the destruction of Jewish life in Germany physically felt through the building's winding design. The building's zigzag outline is often associated with a broken Star of David. The slanted bizarre windows seem to slice through the museum's zinc covering. The organization of the interior rooms is brilliant. There is no clear structure, and empty cement shafts stand in the building like cumbersome barriers. These "voids" recall the brutal extermination of the Jews during the Nazi dictatorship. The modern exhibition (with many interactive elements) covers the vast period from Roman times to the present. A multitude of artifacts and pictures portray the daily life and special role of Jews in Germany. One of Berlin's rare baroque structures, a building from 1734/35 which once served as a court of justice, is incorporated into the museum. Libeskind covered the museum's inner courtyard with an expressive glass roof symbolizing a tabernacle.
The **Jewish Museum Berlin Academy** moved into a former wholesale flower market hall on the other side of Lindenstrasse that was redesigned by Libeskind in 2012.

Lindenstrasse 9–14
Open daily 10am–8pm, Mon 10am–10pm
Tel. 25 99 33 00; www.jmberlin.de

▷ U-Bahn stations Kochstrasse, Hallesches Tor

New zigzag building next to the baroque palace: the Jewish Museum

Recalls the flight from Nazi Germany: the "Garden of Exile"

Shimmering silver: the metal shell of the Libeskind building

Jewish everyday life: permanent exhibition in the busy museum

(Clockwise from top left)

KaDeWe

KaDeWe

Berlin would be unimaginable without the Department Store of the West (Kaufhaus des Westens). The largest department store on the European continent is more than a well-stocked shopping paradise: KaDeWe is a legend. A visit to the grocery store and delicatessen on the top floor should not be missed. This is where an international public can be found feasting on champagne and oysters.

The success of this department store was not foreseeable when it opened on **Wittenbergplatz** in 1907. The architect Emil Schaudt designed the building at Tauentzienstrasse 21–24 to fit the architecture of the nearby middle class residential neighborhood. But with the KaDeWe, the **Tauentzien**, which connects to → **Kurfürstendamm** from the east, rapidly developed into an important shopping mile. In 1929 two more floors were added to the five-story department store. The KaDeWe was again extensively enlarged in the 1990s and an impressive rooftop with a winter garden was added. A "boulevard" of luxury-line products was set up on the ground floor.

Tauentzienstrasse 21–24
www.kadewe.de
▷ U-Bahn station Wittenbergplatz

Visual pleasure: KaDeWe's decorated shop window

Friendly welcome: a porter at the main entrance of the Department Store of the West

Exotic tastes: the food department of the famous department store

Opened its doors in 1907: Berlin's largest shopping paradise

(Clockwise from top left)

KaDeWe

KAUFHAUS DES WESTENS

Karl-Marx-Allee
Karl-Marx-Allee

You don't have to travel far in Berlin to get a small taste of Moscow. The East German state almost identically copied Soviet architecture along about two kilometers of Karl-Marx-Allee (called Stalinallee from 1949–61), which runs east from → **Alexanderplatz**.

When constructions on the "first socialist street in Germany" began under the supervision of Hermann Henselmann in 1952, the residential buildings were rather comfortably, even luxuriously furnished with elevators and parquet flooring. This object of prestige of the young GDR, however, became the nucleus of the workers' uprising on June 17, 1953.

The 90 meter wide avenue between **Strausberger Platz** and Proskauer Strasse was completed in 1961. After reunification, the historical monument was restored bit by bit and the façade was again clad with Meissner ceramic. The towers on **Frankfurter Tor** and the **Kino Kosmos** cinema are two architectural highpoints on Karl-Marx-Allee. The **Kino International** was built in the modernist style near Strausberger Platz in 1965.

▷ U-Bahn stations Strausberger Platz, Frankfurter Tor

Grand building in the Moscow style: historic bookstore on Karl-Marx-Allee

View to Alexanderplatz: the fountain on Strausberger Platz was created in 1967

Resembling the domes at Gendarmenmarkt: residential tower on Frankfurter Tor

Popular cinema on Karl-Marx-Allee: the Kino International

(Clockwise from top left)

NATIONAL

IVG

Kollwitzplatz
Kollwitzplatz

Nowhere else in Berlin are so many restaurants and bars concentrated into a single area: The district of Prenzlauer Berg, once a quarter for common people, has blossomed into a chic, trendy neighborhood. Part of its allure has no doubt to do with the charmingly decorated façades on the almost uninterrupted sea of buildings built during the Gründerzeit era.
From the attractive **Senefelderplatz** with the historic **Pfefferberg** beer garden the slope continues upward to Kollwitzplatz, named after the painter and graphic designer Käthe Kollwitz (1867–1945), who lived there until her death. A copy of her sculpture "Mother with two children" stands in the park.
The **Kulturbrauerei** is located nearby between Knaackstrasse and Schönhauser Allee. The complex from 1889, protected as an historic monument, was designed by Franz Schwechten, who also designed the Memorial Church. Today the original brick halls attract guests to the clubs, movie theaters and restaurants that have been established there.
The **Pratergarten**, Berlin's oldest beer garden from 1837, is nearby on Kastanienallee. The Kastanienallee is particularly "in" at the moment with young people, thanks to its unrenovated appearance. But the transition is already underway.

Kulturbrauerei
Knaackstrasse 97
www.kulturbrauerei-berlin.de

▷ U-Bahn station Eberswalder Strasse

Berlin classic: subway viaduct on Schönhauser Allee

Meeting place for night owls: the Kulturbrauerei

The plaza was named after her: Käthe Kollwitz monument by Gustav Seitz

Restaurants and bars en masse: the area around Kollwitzplatz

(Clockwise from top left)

Kulturforum
Cultural Forum

Right next-door to the area of newly constructed buildings on → **Potsdamer Platz**, Berlin shines with a concentrated presentation of art and culture of international standing. The Cultural Forum on both sides of the Potsdamer Strasse is also one of the most significant building ensembles of the postwar period in West Berlin. From 1959–64, Hans Scharoun developed a concept of spectacular solitary buildings that fuse into a "city landscape." The Philharmonic, Chamber Music Hall, State Library, Painting Gal lery and the New National Gallery form a unique intellectual-cultural center.

The **Philharmonic** was the first of the buildings to be constructed (1960–63). The concert hall with its expressive design is famous throughout the world for its superb acoustics. The Berlin Philharmonic Orchestra (founded in 1882) at

Painting Gallery
Matthäikirchplatz
Tue–Fri 10am–6pm, Thu until 8pm,
Sat/Sun 11am–6pm

New National Gallery
Potsdamer Strasse 50
Closed for general refurbishment until 2019

Tel. (for both) 266 42 42 42; www.smb.museum

Musical Instrument Museum
Tiergartenstrasse 1, entrance at Ben-Gurion-Strasse
Tue–Fri 9am–5pm, Thu until 8pm, Sat/Sun 10am–5pm
Tel. 25 48 11 78; www.mim-berlin.de

St. Mathew's Church
Matthäikirchplatz 1
Tue–Sun 12pm–6pm
Tel. 262 12 02; www.stiftung-stmatthaeus.de

▷ S- and U-Bahn station Potsdamer Platz, bus 200

A collection of cultural sites of international standing: the Cultural Forum

Unifying old and new: Painting Gallery with the St. Mathew's Church

Known for its excellent music: the Chamber Music Hall

Prime location for classical music: Philharmonic (left) and Chamber Music Hall

(Clockwise from top left)

home here is considered one of the world's best classical music orchestras. Scharoun also designed the adjacent **Chamber Music Hall** and **Musical Instrument Museum**, which were realiz ed in 1985–87 by his student, the architect Edgar Wisniewski.

The impressive **NewState Library** (1967–78), which looks like a shiny golden boulder next to the new buildings on Potsdamer Platz, is also worth taking a look at. The transparent **New National Gallery** by Ludwig Mies van der Rohe (built in 1965–68) exhibits 20th century works. The **Painting Gallery** is dedicated to historic painting up to the 18th century. The neighboring redbrick **Museum of Decorative Arts** was designed by Rolf Gutbrod (built in 1979–85). The **St. Mathew's Church**, built by Friedrich August Stüler and located in the middle of the Forum, was a witness to Prussian history.

Temple of art with cult status: the New National Gallery by Mies van der Rohe

Survived the inferno of World War II: St. Mathew's Church by Stüler

Shows famous works by Europe's old masters: the Painting Gallery

(Clockwise from top)

Kurfürstendamm
Kurfürstendamm

The bustling, sophisticated Kurfürstendamm is 3.5 kilometers long, running from the → **Memorial Church** through Berlin's west side. The world famous avenue lined with plane trees was the inspiration of Reich Chancellor Otto von Bismarck. Following his vision, upscale residential villas were built with decorative stately façades beginning in 1886. The elegant "Kudamm" soon developed into a pulsating central axis with cinemas and urban entertainment. Elegant haute couture boutiques are concentrated in the area between Bleibtreustrasse and Adenauerplatz. **Café Kranzler**, the city's most famous coffee house, is located at the intersection to Joachimstaler Strasse. Next to the low 1950s building, Kurfürstendamm reveals its more contemporary side: A semi-circle luxury hotel (with sculptures by Markus Lüpertz) and the glassed-in **Neues Kranzler-Eck** stand diagonally across from one another. The commercial arcade in the Kranzler-Eck leads straight into the loveliest theater building of the Belle Époque: The **Theater des Westens** on Kantstrasse, which opened in 1896, performs light fare, musicals and variety shows.
It is worthwhile taking a little detour along the side street **Fasanenstrasse**. Here stands an urban villa with a garden that has been preserved

Käthe Kollwitz Museum
Fasanenstrasse 24
Open daily 11am–6pm
Tel. 882 52 10; www.kaethe-kollwitz.de

Theater des Westens
Kantstrasse 12
Tel. 31 90 30; www.theater-des-westens.de

▷ U-Bahn stations Kurfürstendamm, Uhlandstrasse or Adenauerplatz

Dynamic: the Neues Kudamm-Eck

Vibrant: Luxury hotel on Joachimstaler Platz

Illuminated: traditional Café Kranzler with the Neues Kranzler-Eck

A green band running through Berlin's west: Kurfürstendamm

(Clockwise from top left)

CONCORDE BERLIN
PASTA
VAPIANO
PIZZA

KRANZLER
GERRY WEBER
LINDEX
LINDEX
LINDEX
LINDEX

from the early days of the Kurfürstendamm. Today the **Literature House** and café (no. 23) is an oasis in the middle of the hectic city. Right next door stands the **Käthe Kollwitz Museum** showing works by the socially critical artist (1867–1945).
The **Jewish Community Center** is located north of Kudamm at Fasanenstrasse 79/80. The synagogue that was dedicated on these same grounds in 1912 burned down during the pogrom night of 1938. The synagogue's original portal survived the fire and now stands at the entrance to the simple structure from 1959.

Upper middle-class urban palace from 1891/92: the Villa Grisebach on Fasanen-strasse

Recalls the synagogue burned down in 1938: Torah scroll sculpture in front of the Jewish community center

Idyllic: Literature House garden café on Fasanenstrasse

Mix of architectural styles: the Theater des Westens

(Clockwise from top left)

Marienkirche
St. Mary's Church

It looks a little lost today among the monumental structures from the GDR era: Standing in the shadow of the → **Television Tower**, St. Mary's Church recalls that a good 800 years ago the core of Berlin existed here, with narrow lanes and small markets.

The gothic house of worship, first documented in 1295, houses a number of outstanding religious treasures. One of them is the historically important "Dance of Death" fresco, which was created in 1484 in the tower hall following a plague epidemic. The baroque alabaster pulpit from 1702/03 was designed by Andreas Schlüter. The copper tower head – a masterpiece of Carl Gotthard Langhans – was added to St. Mary's Church in 1790.

The opulent **Neptune Fountain** stands near the church. Berlin's loveliest fountain from 1888 was a gift from the city to the last German emperor. The work created by the sculptor Reinhold Begas symbolizes the four rivers Rhine, Elbe, Oder and Vistula.

The **Berlin Town Hall**, which also goes back to the early days of the capital, bears the nickname "Red Town Hall" because of its redbrick front. It was built in 1861–69 according to plans by Hermann Friedrich Waesemann. The tower in the northern Italian gothic style is 74 meters high. The Town Hall houses the offices of the Berlin state administration, the Senate and the mayor of Berlin.

Karl-Liebknecht-Strasse 8
Open daily 10am–6pm
Tel. 258 18 51 12; www.marienkirche-berlin.de

▷ S- and U-Bahn Alexanderplatz, bus 100, 200

Famous representatives of Berlin history: St. Mary's Church and the Television Tower

Representing the Berlin population: tower of the Red Town Hall, seat of the Berlin city government

Medieval setting: the bold Neptune Fountain in front of St. Mary's Church

(Clockwise from top)

deine Geschichte!
i.berlin.de
be Berlin

Museumsinsel
Museum Island

One of the most superb museum complexes in all of Europe lies on the northern part of the Spree island in the center of the city: the Museum Island. Over the course of 100 years an ensemble evolved, and by its completion in 1930 five different architects had contributed to its development. The museum district, which was placed on the UNESCO world cultural heritage list in 1999, has been undergoing renovation bit by bit since the end of the 1990s. A new entrance building is also being added.

The **Old Museum**, built by Karl Friedrich Schinkel in 1825–30, was the first museum building to be erected in Berlin. It is a masterpiece of classical architecture with its front dominating the **Lustgarten** at the → **Berlin Cathedral**. The inspiring rotunda, modeled after the Pantheon in Rome, is a fitting prelude to the antique collection on display inside.

The **New Museum** contains the Egyptian Museum with the famous bust of Nefertiti. The reconstruction of the building (re-opened in 2009) that was originally erected by Friedrich August Stüler (1843–46) is a striking mix of

Old Museum
Tue–Sun 10am–6pm, Thu until 8pm

Old National Gallery
Tue–Sun 10am–6pm, Thu until 8pm

Bode Museum
Tue–Sun 10am–6pm, Thu until 8pm

New Museum
Open daily 10am–6pm, Thu until 8pm

Pergamon Museum
Open daily 10am–6pm, Thu until 8pm

Tel. (for all) 266 42 42 42; www.smb.museum

▷ S-Bahn station Hackescher Markt, bus 100, 200

Schinkel's main work: the Old Museum at Lustgarten

Classicism à la Prussia: the Rotunda of the Old Museum

Historic cultural temples on Museum Island: Old National Gallery (right) and New Museum

(Clockwise from top left)

old and new. The **Old National Gallery**, Stüler's second work, stands next to the New Museum. The museum resembles an antique temple elevated on a high pedestal. It displays 19th century German and European painting and sculpture by artists such as Manet, Monet, Renoir, Caspar David Friedrich and Karl Friedrich Schinkel. Stüler's design was completed by Johann Heinrich Strack in 1867–76. The equestrian statue on the staircase portrays King Friedrich Wilhelm IV, who first had the idea for the Museum Island.
The **Bode Museum**, built in 1898–1904 by Ernst von Ihne, forms the northern tip of Museum Island. The museum's collection focuses on religious artwork from Byzantine and European sculpture from the Renaissance to the Baroque era.
Pergamon Museum (built by Alfred Messel in 1907–30) is an undiminished success with the public. Inside visitors can admire the archeological findings of antiquity, the Ishtar Gate from Babylon and the impressive Pergamon Altar.

Housed today in the Old National Gallery: the princesses sculpture by Schadow

Neo-baroque: the Bode Museum on the tip of Museum Island

World famous resident of the New Museum: the Egyptian Queen Nefertiti

The Pergamon Museum's great attraction: the monumental altar from the city of Pergamon in Asia Minor

(Clockwise from top)

Museumszentrum Dahlem

Dahlem Museum Center

In addition to the → **Museum Island** and the → **Cultural Forum** there is a third important location for museums in Berlin: the **Museums of Art and World Cultures** in Dahlem. In the southwest part of Berlin, collections on European and non-European cultures and the **Museum of Ethnology** are exhibited. The collection with 500,000 objects from all over the world is one of the largest worldwide.
The objects in the **Museum for Indian Art** and the **Museum of Asian Art** are superbly displayed. The **Museum of European Cultures**, showing the culture and daily life of German-speaking peoples in Central Europe from the 16th century to the present, is also first-rate. The museum-planner Wilhelm von Bode had the idea for the museum site in 1911. Its implementation, however, was not realized until after World War II. The designs for the modern buildings came from the architects Wils Ebert and Fritz Bornemann.

Museum of Ethnology
Museum of Asian Art
Museum of European Cultures
Lansstrasse 8
Tue–Fri 10am–5pm, Sat/Sun 11am–6pm
Tel. 266 42 42 42; www.smb.museum

▷ U-Bahn station Dahlem Dorf

Colossal: sculptural art by the natives of Middle America

New building in Dahlem: Museums for Art and World Cultures

On display in the Museum of Ethnology: original huts from the South Pacific

(Clockwise from top left)

AFRIKA
AMERIKA
ASIEN
EUROPA
MUSEUM FÜR ASIATISCHE KUNST - MUSEUM EUROPÄISCHER KULTUREN

Neue Synagoge
New Synagogue

The New Synagogue in the Spandauer Vorstadt is one of the most beautiful buildings in Berlin. The more than 150 year old Jewish place of worship was the largest and most important synagogue in all of Germany. After it was partly damaged during World War II, only the building's front section was reconstructed and is used today by the **Centrum Judaicum** (the Jewish culture, documentation, and special events center).
Eduard Knoblauch created the design for the building on Oranienburger Strasse in 1857–59; after the architect's death, August Stüler supervised its construction until 1866. The Moorish-influenced style with the shimmering gold cupola is unique in Berlin. The synagogue's prayer hall, which no longer exists, once seated 3,000. During the pogrom night of 1938, a courageous policeman was able to rescue the New Synagogue from plundering Nazis.
Oranienburger Strasse is a popular place for nightlife. In the **Heckmann-Höfe**, the courtyards next to the synagogue, the charm of the historic quarter has been preserved. The **Postfuhramt** (an old post office on the corner of Tucholskystrasse), built in 1875–81, reflects the architectural style of the synagogue.
The oldest **Jewish Cemetery** in Berlin (1672 to 1827) lies on Grosse Hamburger Strasse. It was desecrated by the Nazis and serves today as a memorial site.

Oranienburger Strasse 28/30
Sun–Thu 10am–6pm, Fri 10am–2pm, March–Oct.
Sun and Mon 10am–8pm, Apr.–Sept. Fri 10am–5pm
Tel. 88 02 83 16; www.cjudaicum.de

▷ S-Bahn station Oranienburger Strasse

Once a lovely government building, now an exhibition hall: the old post office on Oranienburger Strasse

Built as the most magnificent Jewish prayer house in Europe: the New Synagogue with its striking cupola

In memory of one of the most important German philosophers: Mendelssohn's gravestone at the Jewish cemetery on Grosse Hamburger Strasse

Reconstructed: small prayer room in the New Synagogue

(Clockwise from top left)

Nikolaiviertel
Nikolai District

The Nikolai District on the Spree Island is a kind of open air museum of the destroyed old Berlin. Its current appearance goes back to 1987, when Berlin celebrated its 750th anniversary. The small quarter to the west of → **Alexanderplatz**, with its many cafes and restaurants, is dominated by the **St. Nicholas Church**. The oldest existing structure in Berlin today houses a museum for sacral statues. Construction of the church began around 1230; it acquired its current form in the 15th century.

Several historic buildings from the 16th to the 18th century were reconstructed in the Nikolai District. These include the **Ephraim Palace**, the pub **Zum Nussbaum**, the home of Gotthold Ephraim Lessing (1729–81) and the **Knoblauch House** (1759–61), which shows an exhibition on the Biedermeier period and the influential Knoblauch family.

Nearby, the ruins of the **Cloister Church** (after 1250), the baroque **Parochial Church** (1703) and the **Podewils Palace** (1704) bear witness to history.

St. Nicholas Church
Nikolaikirchplatz
Open daily 10am–6pm

Knoblauch House
Poststrasse 23
Tue–Sun 10am–6pm, Wed 12pm–8pm

Ephraim Palace
Poststrasse 16
Tue–Sun 10am–6pm, Wed 12pm–8pm

Tel. (for all) 24 00 21 62;
www.stadtmuseum.de

▷ S- and U-Bahn station Alexanderplatz, U-Bahn station Klosterstrasse

The "loveliest corner of Berlin": the Ephraim Palace from 1766

Almost 800 years old: the St. Nicholas Church with its towers from 1878

Situated in the heart of the capital: the reconstructed Nikolai District

Pure nostalgia: a replica of the inn Zum Nussbaum erected in the Nikolai District in 1985–87.

(Clockwise from top left)

LA RIVA
Spree-Comtess

Oberbaumbrücke
Oberbaum Bridge

Berlin prides itself on having more bridges than Venice. In truth the Spree city has about 1,000 bridges of various historical styles and periods. The Oberbaum Bridge, connecting Friedrichshain and Kreuzberg over the Spree since 1896, is the most elaborately designed bridge. The name refers to a toll bar, the "Oberbaum", that blocked the river here in former times to collect custom duties. Not only street traffic, but also Berlin's oldest subway line crosses it. The supporting structure for the raised train tracks was architecturally clad with mediaeval-looking ornamentation. Otto Stahn created the structure to resemble a castle in Mark Brandenburg.
Berlin's popular culture has established itself on both sides of the river. Countless clubs and discos attract a style-conscious crowd. The music and fashion trade is at home in the **Media-Spree** on the grounds of the former Osthafen. Right next to the Oberbaum Bridge the Universal music company has moved into a converted cold storage warehouse for chicken eggs that dates back to 1928/29.
Schlesische Strasse on the Kreuzberg side is a highly frequented El Dorado for night owls. The architecturally interesting station at **Schlesisches Tor** is as old as its subway line that opened in 1902.

Cool sound from the old cool storage warehouse: the Universal music company's German branch opened its offices near the Oberbaum Bridge in 2002

Daring construction: highly modern hotel on the Media Spree

Harbor city of Berlin: historic warehouses on Osthafen in Friedrichshain

Medieval cover: the bridge's striking towers are modeled after Brandenburg city gates

(Clockwise from top)

Warschauer Strasse

▷ S- and U-Bahn station Warschauer Strasse, U-Bahn station Schlesisches Tor

Olympiastadion
Olympic Stadium

When the final game of the Soccer World Cup was played in the Olympic Stadium on July 9, 2006, the negative connotations of the arena finally dissipated. Exactly 70 years earlier the Olympic Games had been held in the stadium, which stands near the Havel River. The National Socialists used the games and stadium as an international stage for their propaganda. The arena was erected in 1934–36 according to plans by the architect Werner March in the National Socialist monumental style. Today the neighboring "Maifeld," which was used for mass parades, and the 77-meter-high bell tower still convey the originally intended effect. The stadium with seating for 75,000 spectators was completely renovated for the 2006 World Cup. The architects von Gerkan, Marg & Partner designed for it an elaborate new roof (interrupted by the Marathon Gate) with a state-of-the-art lighting system. The tartan track is a glowing shade of blue, the color of Hertha BSC, Berlin's soccer team. Swimming, hockey and riding stadiums stand next to the Olympic Stadium. The **Waldbühne**, a stage set into a 30-meter-deep hollow, is a popular place for outdoor summer concerts.

Visitor Center
Olympischer Platz 3 (at the east gate)
Tel. 25 00 23 22; www.olympiastadion-berlin.de

▷ S- and U-Bahn station Olympiastadion

A roof was added for the Soccer World Cup in 2006: the Olympic Stadium

Built for the 1936 Olympics in the National Socialist architectural style: Germany's largest sports stadium

Popular place for outdoor concerts: the Waldbühne

(Clockwise from top)

Pariser Platz

Pariser Platz

Although Pariser Platz at the → **Brandenburg Gate** has been completely redone since reunification, visitors have the impression that its past was never interrupted.

House Sommer and **House Liebermann**, the new buildings designed by Josef Paul Kleihues that flank the gate, resemble the original buildings by Stüler that were destroyed.

Hotel Adlon also mimics the style of the past. The legendary luxury guest house was rebuilt at its original location. The **Eugen Gutmann House** and the **French Embassy**, designed by Christian de Portzamparc in the style of a palace, make a positive impression on the northern end of Pariser Platz. The south side is occupied by the **Academy of Arts** (next to Hotel Adlon), which received special permission to have a glass front (Günther Behnisch), the **DZ-Bank**, which conceals behind its severe façade the visionary stylistic vocabulary of the world-famous architect Frank O. Gehry, and finally, the **American Embassy**, which opened in 2008 and was the last building to be completed on the plaza (Moore, Ruble, Yudell).

Academy of Arts
Pariser Platz 4
Open daily 8am–10pm
www.adk.de

Max Liebermann House
Pariser Platz 7
Tel. 22 63 30 30; www.stiftung.brandenburgertor.de

▷ S- und U-Bahn station Brandenburger Tor

Fancy: the Hotel Adlon (left) next to the Academy of Arts

From above: Adlon, Academy, DZ-Bank and U.S. Embassy (to the left) on the south front of Pariser Platz

Expressive: inner court of the DZ-Bank

World famous: Brandenburg Gate with the neighboring houses Liebermann (right) and Sommer

(Clockwise from top left)

Pfaueninsel
Peacock Island

Peacock Island is a dreamy isle that will make romantic hearts leap. Every square meter of the Havel island on the west side of the Wannsee was artistically designed. Peter Joseph Lenné, the famous garden designer, created a fairytale landscape in 1820–36 where about 60 peacocks roam about freely today. Karl Friedrich Schinkel built the Cavalier House in 1823 with the gothic façade of a nobleman's house from Danzig.

King Friedrich Wilhelm II (1744–97) discovered the idyllic island as a leisure area and had the little white palace designed to resemble ruins for Wilhelmine Encke, his early love and mistress (1752–1820). The monarch's apartment with all its original furnishings can be seen inside the picturesque love nest from 1794/95.

A path runs along the riverbank of the Havel to another of the Prussian ruling family's estates. The **Glienicke Palace** was designed by Schinkel in 1825–27 in the style of an Italian villa for Prince Carl of Prussia. It is imbedded in an enchanting park that also bears Lenné's signature. The building next door, called Casino, provides a lovely view of the picturesque Havel landscape.

Pfaueninselchaussee 1
Open all year until dusk

▷ S-Bahn station Wannsee, then bus 218

Glienicke Palace
Königstrasse 36
Tue–Sun 10am–6pm, Nov.–March Sat/Sun until 5pm

Both: Tel. 80 58 67 50; www.spsg.de

▷ S-Bahn station Wannsee, then bus 316

Designed by the master builder Schinkel: the Cavalier House on Peacock Island

Erected in 1795 on the north end of the island: the dairy farm with the gothic hall

Glorious estate nearby: Glienicke Palace with Italian style fountain

Romantic island in the Havel river: Peacock Island with the white pleasure palace

(Clockwise from top)

Potsdam

Potsdam, once the residence of the Prussian crown and today the capital of the state of Brandenburg, is world famous thanks to its unique cultural landscape from the time of Frederick the Great (1712–86).
With the **Sanssouci Palace and Park**, the king created a retreat before the gates of Berlin that suited his personal tastes. The estate's special highlight is the splendid Sanssouci Palace ("without worries"), with its gently curving vineyards. It is a masterpiece of rococo built by the architect Georg Wenzeslaus von Knobelsdorff in 1745–47.
The rather modest palace helped establish Frederick's image as the enlightened philosopher-king. His grave lies right next to his beloved palace.
Another rococo treasure here is the **Chinese Teahouse** from 1756. The **New Palace**, which the monarch built in 1763–69 after the Seven Years War, demonstrates the power and greatness of Prussia. The **New Orangery** ensemble emerged in 1851–61 and was modeled after the Italian Renaissance.
Next to Sanssouci lies the **New Garden**, the Hohenzollern's second park grounds. Both the classical **Marble Palace** (1787–91) and the **Cecilienhof Palace** (1913–17) lie on the lake "Heiliger See". The latter building was the venue for the Potsdam Conference that took place in

Tourist Information
Brandenburgische Strasse 3
Tel. 0331/27 55 80; www.potsdamtourismus.de

Park Sanssouci Visitor Center
An der Orangerie 1
Tel. 0331/969 42 00; www.spsg.de

▷ S-Bahn station Potsdam main station

Almost modest: Charlottenhof Palace in the Sanssouci Park

Italian Renaissance in Potsdam: the New Orangery

Highlight of German Rococo: the Sanssouci Palace, Frederick the Great's residence

Golden garden pavilion: the Chinese Teahouse on the palace park grounds

(Clockwise from top)

1945, attended by the victorious powers of World War II.

Both the imposing **St. Nicholas Church** (1830–50) by Karl Friedrich Schinkel, as well as the former **Potsdam City Palace** that was destroyed in 1960, were rebuilt at Alter Markt in the city center. The slightly modified early baroque residence (from 1664–70) from the time of the Great Elector, is the seat of the state parliament of Brandenburg.

The **Dutch Quarter** in the old town (Mittelstrasse) is a charming area established in 1732–42 for immigrants from Holland in the style of their homeland.

Brandenburgische Strasse is the central shopping avenue in Potsdam. At its western end stands the **Brandenburg Gate** in the style of a Roman triumphal arch.

Imported architectural style: the Dutch Quarter was supposed to allure artisans from Holland to Potsdam

This is where the victors of World War II conferred in 1945: the Cecilienhof Palace in the New Garden

Entrance to the old town: Potsdam's Brandenburg Gate from 1770

On the lake Heiliger See: the Marble Palace in the New Garden

(Clockwise from top left)

Potsdamer Platz
Potsdamer Platz

Potsdamer Platz personifies the "New Berlin," the epoch-making transformation of a city divided by a wall into an open metropolis at Europe's center. Over a brief decade at the turn of the millennium, a modern vivacious urban center developed on the vast wasteland left behind by the destruction of war and the construction of the Berlin Wall. Its attractions include a musical theater, casino, first-run cinemas and a shopping mall.

A very busy spot is the "Piazza" in the **Sony Center**, which is protected from weather by a tent-like roof. The spectacular steel and glass construction, a masterpiece created by the architect Helmut Jahn, hovers like a huge umbrella above five buildings. At night the structure is illuminated in candy-colors. The Belle Époque rooms exhibited behind a glass front at the Piazza were once part of the luxury Hotel Esplanade from 1908.

The Berlin film festival (Berlinale), the **Boulevard of Stars** und the **Film Museum** make Potsdamer Platz the primary location for cineasts. The Marlene Dietrich Collection shows the film legacy of the world famous diva (1901–92) from Berlin. Contemporary movie stars often stay at the Ritz-Carlton, the art deco flagship hotel of the elegant **Beisheim Center** that lies on the northern edge of Potsdamer Platz.

A replica of Berlin's first traffic light (1924)

Musical Theater at Potsdamer Platz and **Casino**
Marlene-Dietrich-Platz 1

Museum of Film and Television
Potsdamer Strasse 2
Tue–Sun 10am–6pm, Thu until 8pm
Tel. 300 90 30; www.deutsche-kinemathek.de

▷ S and U-Bahn station Potsdamer Platz

Aiming high: three towers on Potsdamer Platz, buildings from the turn of the millennium

Unforgotten: star for Marlene Dietrich on the Boulevard of Stars

Show stage: Marlene-Dietrich-Platz with the Musical Theater and Casino

Grandiose: the stunning roof of the Sony Center illuminated in trendy colors

(Clockwise from top left)

can be found on Potsdamer Platz. Traffic was navigated from this tower to the neighboring **Leipziger Platz**, whose octagonal form dating from 1734 now accommodates captivating contemporary architecture, such as the Mall of Berlin shopping center that opened in 2014. The **German Bundesrat**, parliament's upper house, convenes at Leipziger Strasse 3/4 in an historic plenary building from 1901–04 that used to be the seat of the Prussian House of Lords.

Once a symbol of a fast-paced Berlin: traffic light from 1924

Film stars and VIPs from all over the world reside here: the Ritz-Carlton (left) in the Beisheim Center

Meeting place for the German Bundesrat: the former Prussian House of Lords

Opened on the nearby Leipziger Platz in 2014: The Mall of Berlin shopping center

(Clockwise from top left)

BAHNHOF POTSDAMER PLATZ
DB

DEICHMAN

BUNDESRAT

Regierungsviertel
Government Quarter

Germany's political heart beats at the Spreebogen, north of the → **Tiergarten**. The **Bundestag** and **Federal Chancellery** form an urban ensemble here that was developed at the turn of the millennium. The impressive new buildings of the Government Quarter are lined up right next to the time-honored → **Reichstag Building**.

First occupied in May 2001, the chancellery on the bank of the Spree is one of Berlin's most prominent architectural structures. With its unconventional columns, the 36-meter-high façade of the court of honor resembles an expressive stage set. Huge openings on both sides of the main building imbue the power headquarters with an air of transparency. The long side wings contain 310 offices for the staff working for the head of government. The complex and park on this side of the Spree were designed by Axel Schultes and Charlotte Frank.

The same architects designed the arrangement of the other large Bundestag offices: the **Paul Löbe Building** (next to the Reichstag Building) and the **Marie Elisabeth Lüders Building** (on the opposite bank of the Spree), which appear buoyant and fanciful where they cross the Spree. The path along the river offers an attractive panoramic view. Stephan Braunfels designed the buildings which house the committee con-

Bundestag
Visitor Services
Platz der Republik 1
Tel. 22 73 21 52; www.bundestag.de

Federal Chancellery
Willy-Brandt-Strasse 1
www.bundesregierung.de

▷ U-Bahn station Bundestag

Spectacular: the front of the Federal Chancellery

Staircase to power: stairs leading to the executive suites in the Chancellery's central block

Major round: Cabinet Hall on the six floor of the Chancellery

The power on the Spree: Paul Löbe Building (right) and Reichstag Building

(Clockwise from top left)

ference rooms and Bundestag library. The **Jakob Kaiser Building**, a complex of several buildings on both sides of Dorotheenstrasse, also belongs to the Bundestag.
The **Swiss Embassy** that has resided at Otto-von-Bismarck-Allee 4 since 1919 remains a curiosity. The consulate of Switzerland survived all the historic upheavals in Berlin and is now neighbor to the Federal Chancellery. The old building from 1870 was expanded by the Basel architects Diener & Diener.

Politics' grand stage: the Marie Elisabeth Lüders Building on the northern bank of the Spree

Lined up into the "federal ribbon": Chancellery, Löbe Building and Lüders Building (from top)

No fear of contact: people are comfortable being close to politics in Berlin – as seen here on the Spree bank in front of the Chancellery

(Clockwise from top left)

Corona Extra
Corona Extra

Reichstagsgebäude
Reichstag Building

The Reichstag Building, situated in the → **Government Quarter**, just a few steps from the **Brandenburg Gate**, is the symbol of the Berlin capital. Since April 19, 1999, the German Bundestag has been convening in the parliament building that goes back to the time of the emperor. The 120-year-old building was redesigned and modernized to accommodate parliament's move to the Spree after 50 years in Bonn.
It is the new cupola on the roof of the Reichstag Building that attracts so many visitors. The 800 ton steel and glass structure has a 40 meter high viewing platform that can be reached by traversing two spiral ramps. There is also a rooftop restaurant for visitors.
The 300 million Euro renovations were planned by the British architect Sir Norman Foster. Placing importance on ecological construction methods, he designed the huge reflecting cylinder in the middle of the cupola to funnel light into the plenary chamber below.
The Reichstag Building was originally built in 1884–94 to plans by Paul Wallot, but was destroyed in the Reichstag fire of February 1933.

Platz der Republik 1
Cupola: Open daily 8am–10pm
Besucherdienst
Tel. 22 73 21 25; www.bundestag.de

▷ U-Bahn station Bundestag

Seat of the German Bundestag: the Reichstag Building, built in the Wilhelminian era

One of the most popular attractions in the capital: the glass cupola of the Reichstag Building

From the end of World War II: inscriptions from Soviet soldiers in the corridors of the building

High-tech within old walls: plenary hall in the remodeled Reichstag Building

(Clockwise from top left)

Schloss Bellevue
Bellevue Palace

Spreeweg 1 is the postal address of the Federal President. Spreeweg 1 is also the address of the Bellevue Palace, which since the 1950s has served as the Berlin residence of the head of state and since 1994 as his main and only office. The three-wing structure at the upper west edge of the → **Tiergarten** was built for the youngest brother of Frederick the Great, the regent prince Ferdinand of Prussia. Philipp Daniel Boumann provided the designs for the classical palace that was built in 1785/86. The façade resembles the original, but the rooms of the interior were redesigned when the building was reconstructed after the World War.

The president's staff works in a new building set 100 meters to the south of the palace. Martin Gruber and Helmut Kleine-Kraneburg designed the building with the dark gray-green façade of natural stone. The oval shape of the mere 15-meter-high **Federal President's Office** has led to its nickname: "president's egg." Thanks to its unusual form, all the office windows face the park.

Spreeweg 1
www.bundespraesident.de

▷ S-Bahn station Bellevue, bus 100

Once the residence of the Prussian nobility, now the official residence of the federal president: Bellevue Palace

Set amidst nature: palace and park grounds lie idyllically within the Tiergarten

"President's egg": the head of state's staff works in the President's Office, not far from the palace

(Clockwise from top)

Schloss Charlottenburg
Charlottenburg Palace

Not far from the West-City lie the largest palace grounds in Berlin. The baroque Charlottenburg Palace reflects in nuances the history of the ruling Hohenzollern dynasty. High-quality art museums of classic modernism can also be found all around the Prussian residence.
In 1695–99 the central middle section with eleven window axes was built by Johann Arnold Nering. The building was used as a summer palace for the Electress Sophie Charlotte (1668–1705) and named in her honor. The palace was enlarged by the architect Johann Friedrich Eosander von Göthe from 1701 to 1712, which was also when the bold tower, the long side wings around the court of honor and, further west, the Orangery, were added.
The Prussian king Frederick the Great (1712–86) had Wenzeslaus von Knobelsdorff design the New Wing (1740–46) as an eastern counter-

Spandauer Damm 10–22
Old Palace: Tues–Sun 10am–6pm, Nov.–March until 5pm
New Wing: Wed–Mon 10am–6pm, Nov.–March until 5pm
Tel. 32 09 11; www.spsg.de

Berggruen Museum
Schlossstrasse 1

Scharf-Gerstenberg Collection
Schlossstrasse 70
Tue–Fri 10am–6pm, Sat/Sun 11am–6am

Tel. (both) 266 42 42 42; www.smb.museum.de

Bröhan Museum
Schlossstrasse 1a
Tue–Sun 10am–6pm
Tel. 32 69 06 00; www.broehan-museum.de

▷ U-Bahn station Richard-Wagner-Platz, bus M 45

Majestic residence of Prussian kings: Charlottenburg Palace

Finest Baroque: together palace and park form an artistic ensemble

The monarchs' exuberant collection: the porcelain cabinet is a highlight of Charlottenburg Palace

(Clockwise from top)

point. The most recent change was a theater, created by Carl Gotthard Langhans and added to the Orangery in 1788–91.
The rooms of the palace are furnished in various baroque, rococo und classical styles. The palace park displays a baroque landscape design. The **Mausoleum**, which contains the grave monument of the popular Queen Luise (1776–1810), is hidden within the expansive grounds. The **equestrian statute of the Great Elector** in the court of honor was created by Andreas Schlüter around 1700 and is considered one of the most important equestrian monuments of the baroque period.
Three superb museums are located across from the palace on Schlossstrasse: the **Berggruen Museum** with a large Picasso collection, the **Scharf-Gerstenberg Collection** with classical modernist and surrealist painting, and the **Bröhan Museum**, displaying crafts in the Jugendstil, art déco and functionalist styles.

Masterpiece by Christian Daniel Rauch: the grave sculpture "Queen Luise" in the Charlottenburg mausoleum

On horseback: equestrian statue of the Great Elector in the palace's court of honor

Modern interior in an old building: stairwell in the Berggruen Museum

Visiting the Stüler building across from the palace: the Berggruen Museum with a first-class Picasso collection

(Clockwise from top left)

Schloss Köpenick

Köpenick Palace

Palace fans will find it worthwhile to take a trip to Berlin's outer district of Köpenick. The palace on the edge of the old town is the most important structure in Berlin from the time of the Great Elector (1620–88). It was enlarged in 1677–90 for his successor Frederick III (1657–1713), who later became the first king of Prussia. Master builder Rutger van Langervelt designed the palace in the style of Dutch baroque. The palace church by Johann Arnold Nering was erected in 1685.

The palace, today the **Museum of Decorative Arts**, exhibits the Hohenzollern's impressive treasures and the richly ornamented coat of arms room from 1685.

In 1730 a spectacular trial took place in the palace. Crown Prince Frederick (1712–86), later known as "the Great," was tried as a deserter before a military court for his planned escape to England. He was granted amnesty, but his friend and helper, Lieutenant von Katte, was executed before his eyes in Küstrin. Köpenick became known beyond Berlin's borders through the surprise coup of the cobbler Wilhelm Voigt, who clad in a military uniform, confiscated the town hall treasury in 1906. The famous Captain of Köpenick is commemorated in an exhibit at the crime site.

Museum of Decorative Arts
Schlossinsel 1
Thu–Sun 11am–5pm
Tel. 266 42 42 42; www.smb.museum

Köpenick Town Hall
Alt-Köpenick 21
Mon–Fri 10am–6pm

▷ S-Bahn station Köpenick or Spindlersfeld, then tram 60, 62

Set on a peninsula near the old town of Köpenick: Köpenick Palace

Köpenick cult figure: the captain of Köpenick is honored with a statue at the town hall

Opulently designed coat of arms room with porcelain of Frederick the Great: the palace is used as a museum of decorative arts

(Clockwise from top)

Siegessäule
Victory Column

The Victory Column at **Grosser Stern** is – after the Brandenburg Gate and the Television Tower – the most well-known landmark of Berlin. The 69-meter-high cylinder has partially the Love Parade to thank for its popularity. For many years the end party was celebrated at the plaza around the Victory Column.
The Victory Column was originally dedicated to acts of war. The monument, built by Johann Heinrich Strack (1865–73), recalls Prussian victories over Denmark, Austria and France in 1864, 1866 and 1870/71. This is the reason it is decorated with gilded gun barrels. The colorful mosaic by Anton von Werner in the column gallery glorifies the war against France and the founding of the German Reich in 1871.
The heroic pose of the 8.32-meter-high winged goddess of victory, by Friedrich Drake, is also unmistakable. But the Berliners can no longer relate to the national gesture – and disrespectfully refer to the Victoria as "Golden Else." There are 285 steps to climb to pay her a visit at the tip of the columns, but from there you'll have a fantastic view of the largest park in Berlin, the → **Tiergarten**, and of the neighboring → **Bellevue Palace**.

Grosser Stern
April–Oct. Mon–Fri 9:30am–6:30pm, Sat/Sun until 7pm; Nov.–March Mon–Fri 10am–5pm, Sat/Sun until 5:30pm

▷ bus 100

Symbols of the Reich's founding: Bismarck Monument from 1901 and Victory Column

View over the Tiergarten: Victory Column in front of the President's Office and Bellevue Palace

Prussia's glorious victories: reliefs on the base of the Victory Column recall battles of the 19th century

(Clockwise from top left)

Tempelhofer Flugfeld
Tempelhof Airfield

The former **Tempelhof Airport** became a legend and wrote civilian air traffic history. It was the forefather of all airports in Germany. Opening in 1923, it soon became the busiest airport in Europe. The current complex was built in 1936–41 following plans by Ernst Sagebiel. The huge grounds are an architectural legacy of the Nazi era.
During the blockade of West Berlin in 1948/49, the "Raisin Bomber" planes landed here, sometimes in one-minute intervals, allowing the western Allies to deliver provisions to the closed-off half of the city. The airlift monument on the front plaza recalls this historic assistance.
The airport was closed down to all air traffic in the fall of 2008. Since then this modern aviation monument has been used for major events and fashion shows. The expansive airfield is the largest open grounds in Berlin. The former take-off and landing runways are a Mecca for bikers, strollers and kite skaters.
In the north the airfield is bordered by a typical Berlin district with apartment buildings from the Gründerzeit era. The urban dwellers meet here in cafés and restaurants along **Bergmannstrasse** and **Marheinekeplatz**. Berlin's largest mosque stands on Columbiadamm. The **Sehitlik Mosque**, designed in the classic Ottoman style, was completed in 2005. The two minarets extend 33 meters high.

Platz der Luftbrücke

▷ U-Bahn station Platz der Luftbrücke

Sehitlik Mosque
Columbiadamm 128
Tel. 692 11 18; www.sehitlik-camii.de

▷ bus 104

People instead of planes: former runway of the Tempelhof Airport

Today people sail on the ground: wind skaters on the airfield

Islam is a part of Berlin: the Sehitlik Mosque on the traditional Turkish cemetery near the airport grounds

No flights: all is quiet at the city airport terminal since 2008

(Clockwise from top left)

NEILPRYDE

HAFEN

Tiergarten
Tiergarten

Berlin is a very green metropolis. The city's largest and oldest park is the Tiergarten. A number of attractions are grouped around the centrally-located oasis with an enormous expanse of 210 hectares.

The 500-year-old natural area served as hunting grounds for the aristocracy until 1718. The game reserve was transformed into a park under Frederick the Great (1712–86). The Tiergarten's characteristically natural appearance goes back to the design of the landscape gardener Peter Joseph Lenné: In 1833–39 he created a public park in the English style. The rhododendron grove is from the post-war era. The Floraplatz and Goldfish Pond southwest of the → **Brandenburg Gate** are from the time of Frederick the Great. The "Amazon riding a horse" sculpture was mounted on Floraplatz in 1906. The music monument at the pond in honor of Beethoven, Haydn and Mozart is similarly old. The Luise Island is enchantingly arranged with the monument erected in 1880 for the charismatic Queen Luise. The imposing Wagner Monument (1903) stands on the southern edge of the park. The Goethe Monument (1880) can be found on Ebertstrasse. The → **Victory Column** stands at Grosser Stern.

The **House of World Cultures** on the northern edge of the park is a monument to modernism. The convention hall on John-Foster-Dulles-Allee

Bauhaus Archive
Klingelhöferstrasse 14
Wed–Mon 10am–5pm
Tel. 254 00 20; www.bauhaus.de

▷ bus 100, 200
▷ Park: S-Bahn station Tiergarten or Bellevue, S- and U-Bahn station Brandenburger Tor

A huge oasis in the middle of the city: the Tiergarten

Neo-baroque: Musician's Monument by Rudolf Siemering

A highlight of garden art: the Luise Island on the southern edge of the park

Copy: the "Amazon riding a horse" by Louis Tuaillon on Floraplatz – the original is found on Museum Island

(Clockwise from top left)

was designed by the American architect Hugh Stubbins in 1957.

The **Tiergarten Quarter** begins south of the park. Around the year 2000 an embassy quarter emerged here with extravagant architecture from all over the world. The **Bauhaus Archive** on Landwehrkanal provides information about the epoch-making influence of the art school that existed from 1919–33. Bauhaus founder Walter Gropius designed the museum where the architecture, design and art of this creative think tank is exhibited.

"Pregnant Oyster": the House of World Cultures with the sculpture "Large Butterfly" by Henry Moore

Designed by Walter Gropius personally: the Bauhaus Archive

Asian exotic in the Tiergarten Quarter: the Embassy of the United Arab Emirates

Spectacular façade: the Mexican Embassy

(Clockwise from top)

Unter den Linden

Unter den Linden

The elegant boulevard of the capital and majestic center of the former Prussian metropolis: The avenue Unter den Linden is the city's oldest promenade and stretches all the way from the → **Brandenburg Gate** to the Schlossbrücke (Palace Bridge) and → **Berlin Cathedral.** The first trees were planted in 1647 on orders of the Great Elector (1620–88). The middle strip of the 60 meter wide avenue ends in the east at the **equestrian statue of King Frederick the Great** (1840–51 by Christian Daniel Rauch). We have "old Fritz" to thank that the "Linden" was enlarged into a majestic axis.
After 1740, on what is today Bebelplatz, the **Forum Fridericianum** was established: the State Opera, the Catholic St. Hedwig's Cathedral, the Royal Library and the palace which preceded the Humboldt University. The **State Opera** house (1742 from Knobelsdorff) was enlarged by the younger Carl Ferdinand Langhans after the fire of 1843. The **St. Hedwig's Cathedral** of the diocese of Berlin (1747–73) was modeled after the Pantheon in Rome. The curved **Royal Library** (1780) is today a university institute building. In 1766 a palace was added for one of Frederick II's brothers; it has served as the seat of the **Humboldt University** since 1810. The **Armory** (Zeughaus, 1695–1731 by Andreas

German Historical Museum
Unter den Linden 2
Open daily 10am–6pm
Tel. 20 30 44 44; www.dhm.de

St. Hedwig's Cathedral
Bebelplatz
Mon–Sat 10am–5pm, Sun 1pm–5pm
Tel. 203 48 10; www.hedwigs-kathedrale.de

▷ S- and U-Bahn st. Brandenburger Tor, bus 100, 200

Prussia's grand boulevard: the Unter den Linden avenue runs from the Lustgarten (front right) to the Brandenburg Gate

Prussia's most famous ruler: equestrian statue of Frederick the Great

Prussia's guests: a good resting place beneath linden trees on the center promenade

Prussia's first detached theater: the State Opera House on Unter den Linden

(Clockwise from top left)

Schlüter and others) was built before this construction boom began. The baroque building on the Schlossbrücke, where the **German Historical Museum** resides today, acquired an extension designed by the American architect Ieoh Ming Pei. The **New Guardhouse** (Neue Wache), next to the Armory, was built by Karl Friedrich Schinkel (1818) and is today a national memorial with a Pietà by Käthe Kollwitz. The **Schlossbrücke** at the end of the Linden avenue was also built by Schinkel (1824). Also worth viewing are the **Crown Prince Palace** (no. 3), which was classically remodeled in 1857, and the **Old State Library** (no. 8) by Ernst von Ihne, which opened in 1914. The **Russian Embassy** (no. 55–65) is a magnificent postwar building, a legacy of the former Soviet Union.

Two in one: the German Historical Museum consists of the Pei extension from 2003 and the Armory

Named after the brothers Alexander and Wilhelm von Humboldt: Berlin's oldest university

Today the central memorial for the victims of war and tyranny: the New Guardhouse by Schinkel

The name "Kommode" goes back to its curved form: the Royal Library on Bebelplatz, today part of the Humboldt University

(Clockwise from top left)

HUMBOLDT-UNIVERSITAET
ALEXANDER
VON
HUMBOLDT
AL SEGUNDO DESCUBRIDOR DE CUBA
LA UNIVERSIDAD DE LA HABANA 1939

Wilhelmstrasse

Wilhelmstrasse

At one time Germany's national leadership was concentrated on Wilhelmstrasse, a street running south from the → **Government Quarter**.
A government district since the Bismarck era, its grounds were expanded into a center of power under the Nazi dictatorship.
Historic buildings from this dark epoch include the huge office complex south of Leipziger Strasse. Erected in 1935/36 according to plans by Ernst Sagebiel, it was to serve as the Reich Ministry of Aviation where Germany prepared for war. Today the massive structure is called the **Detlev Rohwedder Building** and houses the Federal Ministry of Finance.
The Gestapo and SS had their headquarters on the grounds across the street, where they held political prisoners in basement cells that have been partially preserved. The exhibition **"Topography of Terror"** provides information about the regime in power from 1933–45.
The preserved section of the Berlin Wall along Niederkirchnerstrasse makes clear the connection between World War II and the subsequent division of Germany.
Changing exhibitions are shown in the **Martin Gropius Building** (1877–81), which is elaborately decorated with mosaics and terracotta.

Topography of Terror
Niederkirchnerstrasse 8
Open daily 10am–8pm
Tel. 25 45 09 50; www.topographie-des-terrors.de

Martin Gropius Building
Niederkirchnerstrasse 7
Wed–Mon 10am–7pm
Tel. 25 48 60; www.gropiusbau.de

▷ U-Bahn station Mohrenstrasse

Legacy of the East German regime: remains of the Berlin Wall on Niederkirchnerstrasse

Legacy of the Hitler regime: the Detlev Rohwedder Building houses the Federal Finance Ministry

Documentation Center on the murderous system of Nazi tyranny: Topography of Terror

Unique architectural monument: the Martin Gropius Building

(Clockwise from top left)

Zitadelle Spandau
Spandau Citadel

The only remaining Renaissance fortress in Northern Europe is located in Spandau, which during the time of its construction was still an independent city outside the gates of Berlin. The Spandau Citadel, the oldest secular building in Berlin, was built in its current form in the 16th century. Certain sections, such as the Julius Tower, which dates back to the early 13th century and the Palas, the residential building from the 14th century, are older. Excavations of the predecessor building – a Slavic castle from the 11th century – still exist. The artistic builder Karl Friedrich Schinkel had the top of the 30-meter-high tower crenellated in 1838. The massive structure, set at the point where the Spree flows into the Havel, was built to secure the trading route from the Rhineland across Magdeburg through Spandau to Poland. Elector Joachim II Hektor (1535–71) resolved to have the citadel enlarged to protect the up and coming city of Berlin. Rochus Graf zu Lynar, a specialist for fortress structures, supervised the work in 1578. The defensive castle, highly modern for its time with sharply angled bastions on each of its four corners, was only directly involved in battle once: In 1813 Napoleon's troops barricaded themselves in here and were fired upon by Prussian military divisions. Today the citadel, completely surrounded by water, is used for cultural events. The grounds also contain museums that tell the history of the fortress and Spandau.

Am Juliusturm 64
Open daily 10am–5pm
Tel. 345 94 40; www.zitadelle-spandau.de

▷ U-Bahn station Zitadelle

Dining in a rustic atmosphere: the "Zitadellen Schänke"

Testimony to the Renaissance: Prince's room in the gatehouse of the citadel

Picturesque: entrance to the citadel with medieval Julius Tower

Oldest secular building in Berlin: the Spandau Citadel

(Clockwise from top left)

Zoologischer Garten
Zoological Garden

Berliners have an intimate relationship to animals. It is no surprise then that the Zoological Garden, with its long history, lies in the center of the City-West. About 17,000 animals romp about within an area of 34 hectares, right next to the train station of the same name and the → **Memorial Church**. It is one of the most interesting zoos in the world with one of the largest collection of animals and over 1552 different species (including the **aquarium**).
The memory of Knut (2006–11), the polar bear who became world famous after his birth in the enclosure, remains strong.
This animal kingdom, founded in 1844 on the initiative of the natural scientists Alexander von Humboldt and Martin Lichtenstein, was the first zoo to be established in Germany. With the help of the landscape designer Peter Joseph Lenné and prominent architects, the grounds were attractively arranged with an Antelope House (1872) and Persian Tower (1910) for equine animals. The entrances on Hardenbergplatz (**Lion's Gate**) and the Budapester Strasse (**Elephant's Gate**) are small works of art from around 1900.

Budapester Strasse 32
Hardenbergplatz 8
March 26–Oct. 14 open daily 9am–7pm; Oct. 15–March 25 open daily 9am–5pm

Aquarium
Budapester Strasse 32
Open daily 9am–6pm

Tel. 25 40 14 00; www.zoo-berlin.de

▷ S- and U-Bahn st. Zoologischer Garten, bus 100

Berlin's favorite child: panda bear in the Zoological Garden

Attractive entrance to the zoo: the Elephant Gate

Plenty of room: the giraffes roam within a spacious outdoor enclosure

Ultra-modern accommodations: the Hippopotamus House

(Clockwise from top left)

Practical Information

BERLIN AREA CODE

When calling from outside Berlin dial the area code 030.

BERLIN INFO

The best and most detailed Internet site on Berlin is the capital's own portal www.berlin.de. The website, which is also presented in English, offers information on hotels, accommodations, current events, transportation and much more.
Detailed information and direct assistance (in booking hotels, bus tours, etc.) is available through Berlin Tourist at www.visitberlin.de (in many languages). Inquiries, ticket sales and booking accommodations can also be made by phone: Tel. 25 00 25.
Three additional "Berlin Tourist Info" offices are open to the public: at the Brandenburg Gate (southern gatehouse, Pariser Platz, open daily 10am–6pm, extended hours from April–Oct.); at the Main Station (Hauptbahnhof, entrance on Europaplatz, open daily 8am–10pm) and in the City-West (Neues Kranzler-Eck, Kurfürstendamm 22, Mon–Sat 10am–8pm, Sun 10am–6pm).

CHOOSING A HOTEL

In addition to Berlin Tourist and the Internet site www.berlin.de (see Berlin Info), the website www.berlin-hotelverzeichnis.de is also helpful in finding and booking suitable accommodations.
Berlin offers a large selection of rooms in different categories. In comparison to other large cities in Europe, rates range from moderate to very inexpensive (on average about 60 euros for a single room).

CURRENT EVENTS

Every two weeks two city magazines Tip and Zitty publish a complete entertainment guide (culture, cinema, music, nightlife, etc) for all of Berlin. The information including a detailed address index (with restaurants) is also accessible online at www.tip-berlin.de and www.zitty.de. A very good program guide and tips on nightlife, clubs, etc. is also found at www.berlin030.de and www.berlinonline.de.

TICKETS

Tickets to cultural events can be booked online at www. berlin.de (culture & tickets) and www. berlinonline.de.
Tickets are also available at the Berlin Tourist shops (see Berlin Info), at Hekticket (Karl-Liebknecht-Strasse 12, 10178, Mitte, Tel. 230 99 30, www.hekticket.de), on the ground floor of the Alexanderplatz station (Dircksenstrasse, 10178, Mitte) and at Ber-ticket.de in the Friedrichstrasse station (exit at Reichstagufer, 10177, Mitte, Tel. 22 48 73 25).

FIRST AID, LOST AND FOUND

Police/emergency assistance: Tel. 110; Fire dept./emergency rescue: Tel. 112; medical assistance/pharmacy after-hours service: Tel. 31 00 31; telephone information: Tel. 118 33; Central lost and found (Platz der Luftbrücke 6, 12101, Tempelhof): Tel. 75 60 31 01; BVG (subway/bus/tram) lost and found (Potsdamer Str. 180–182, 10783, Schöneberg): Tel. 194 49.

CITY TOURS

Bus tours
Most bus tours begin at Alexanderplatz (Alexanderstrasse), Breitscheidplatz (between Meineckestrasse and Rankestrasse) and at Unter den Linden/at the corner of Friedrichstrasse. The City-Circle-Sightseeing tour bus stops at 14 stations and passengers can get on and off. Busses depart every 15 minutes.

Boat tours
There is a large selection of boat tours available including routes through the city center or day-trips to outlying areas. The main boarding docks (with schedules) in the city center are: Jannowitzbrücke, Schlossbrücke (Unter den Linden), Berlin Cathedral, Weidendammer Brücke (Friedrichstrasse) Moltkebrücke (Main Station) and Charlottenburg Schlossbrücke (Bonhoefferufer, Charlottenburger Ufer); in the outlying districts: Tegel, Greenwichpromenade; Zehlendorf, Wannsee.
Because of the large number of different tours and boarding docks, it is wise to contact the boat company directly for information. The two largest companies are Stern- und Kreisschifffahrt (Tel. 5363600) and Reederei Riedel (Tel. 693 46 46).

Walking tours
Here is a small selection of the many companies offering tours (tours vary from traditional sightseeing tours to theme-oriented walks):
www.berlinkompakt.com (Tel. 74 69 44 19), www.berlin-erleben-info.de (Tel. 86 31 36 46), www.berlin-entdecken.de (Tel. 31 80 37 05).
English tours are offered by www.berlinwalks.de (Tel. 301 91 94).
Walks tailored to individual interests at: www.jodock.de (Tel. 61 28 05 37) and www.minoy.de (Tel. 75 47 95 17).
Bike tours through the city are also available: www.berlinonbike.de (Tel. 43 73 99 99), www.fahrradstation.de (Tel. 28 38 48 48); in English: www.fattirebiketoursberlin.com (Tel. 24 04 79 91).

PUBLIC TRANSPORTATION

S-Bahn, U-Bahn, Tram and Bus
Berlin has a very dense public transportation system that covers the entire metropolitan area with S-Bahn, U-Bahn, tram and bus lines. A number of regional trains also serve the suburbs. Schedules and routes are posted at the station stops. Starting at 1am, public transportation at night is provided by busses (ca. every half hour). Hackescher Markt and Zoologischer Garten are the main transfer points for night busses. The main U- and S-Bahn lines run all night from Friday to Sunday.
All public transportation can be used with the same ticket. The local transportation system is divided into three price zones. (A: city center, B: outlying districts, C: outskirts). Tickets must be validated before boarding.
There are attractive time cards available for tourists:

Thee CityTourCard is good throughout the entire city zone (Zone AB) for either 48 or 72 hours and also provides discounts on 30 different cultural and tourist activities. The CityTourCard 48 costs ca. 18 euros; the CityTourCard 72 costs ca. 25 euros. The WelcomeCard (Zone AB plus 200 discounts) is slightly more expensive: 48 hours cost ca. 20 euros, 72 hours cost ca. 27 euros. There is also a 5-day pass available for 32 or 35 euros depending on the special offers.
The bus lines 100 and 200 travel past many sightseeing attractions in the city center; they are a good way to get an impression of the city.
Information about the Berlin transportation system is available at www.bvg.de (BVG info service, Tel. 194 49) and www.s-bahn-berlin.de (S-Bahn customer service, Tel. 29 74 33 33).

Velotaxis
In addition to the normal taxis, velotaxis are also available in Berlin. These modern rickshaw bikes travel along four routes (Kurfürstendamm, Tiergarten, Potsdamer Platz, Unter den Linden). Private tours are available at an extra charge (Tel. 0800/83 56 82 94, www.velotaxi.de).

Cars

The entire inner-city area of Berlin is off-limits to cars emitting high levels of pollutants. Only cars displaying the green low-emission sticker may enter the environmental zone. Motorbikes, motorcycles and vehicles for the disabled are exempted from this regulation. Cars from other countries are also required to display a sticker if they travel within the environmental zone. This designated zone applies to the entire Berlin inner city – the area within the S-Bahn ring (with the exception of the expressway).
Rental car companies are listed on the Internet site www.berlin.de.

Bikes

In addition to several private bike rental companies (Fahrradstation, Dorotheenstrasse 30, Tel. 28 38 48 40, www.fahrradstation.com), Berlin also has the "Call a Bike" service provided by the Deutsche Bahn railway company. More information at www.callabikeinteraktiv.de. Telephone registration is also possible: Tel. 070 00/522 55 22. "Call a Bike" bikes can be found at all the important areas in the city.

CULTURE

Theaters

Berlin is famous for its very diverse theater landscape that unifies both traditional and experimental productions. The *Berliner Ensemble* (Bertolt-Brecht-Platz 1, 10117, Mitte, www.berliner-ensemble.de) under the direction of Claus Peymann, is one of Berlin's most important stages. The *Deutsches Theater* (Schumannstr. 13a, 10117, Mitte, www.deutschestheater.de) is the city's most venerable theater. The small *Maxim Gorki Theater* (Am Festungsgraben 2, 10117, Mitte, www.gorki.de) is a popular favorite. The *Schaubühne* enjoys testing new directions (Kurfürstendamm 153, 10709, Wilmersdorf, www.schaubuehne.de). The *Volksbühne* (Rosa-Luxemburg-Platz 2, 10178, Mitte, www.volksbuehne-berlin.de) is always good for a surprise. *Hebbel am Ufer*, called HAU, (Stresemannstrasse 29, 10963, Kreuzberg, www.hebbel-am-ufer.de) is the main stage for unconventional productions.
Theater am Kurfürstendamm (Kurfürstendamm 209, 10719, Charlottenburg, www.theater-am-kurfuerstendamm.de) and the *Renaissance-Theater* (Knesebeckstrasse 100, 10623, Charlottenburg, www.renaissance-theater.de) offer light comedy.
Grips Theater (Altonaer Strasse 22, 10557, Mitte, www.grips-theater.de) is legendary for its youth and children's productions.

Cabarets, Variety Shows and Musicals

The large commercial theaters include: *Theater am Potsdamer Platz* (Marlene-Dietrich-Platz 1, 10785, Mitte, www.stage-entertainment.de), *Theater des Westens* (Kantstrasse 12, 10623, Charlottenburg, www.stage-entertainment.de) and *Friedrichstadtpalast* (Friedrichstrasse 107, 10117, Mitte, www.friedrichstadtpalast.de).
Political cabaret is offered by the *Distel* (Friedrichstrasse 101, 10117, Mitte, www.distel-berlin.de), *Die Stachelschweine* (Europacenter, Tauentzienstrasse, 10789, Charlottenburg, www.diestachelschweine.de) and the *Wühlmäuse* at Theodor-Heuss-Platz (Pommernallee 2, 14052, Charlottenburg, www.wuehlmaeuse.de).
High-quality cabaret is performed at the *Admiralspalast* (Friedrichstrasse 101, 10178, Mitte, www.admiralspalast.de), *Bar jeder Vernunft* (Schaperstrasse 24, 10719, Wilmersdorf, www.bar-jeder-vernunft.de), *BKA-Theater* (Mehringdamm 34, 10961, Kreuzberg, www.bka-theater.de), *Chamäleon-Varieté* (Hackesche Höfe, Rosenthaler Str. 40/41, 10178, Mitte, www.chamaeleonberlin.de), *Quatsch Comedy Club* (Friedrichstrasse 107, 10117, Mitte, www.quatschcomedyclub.de) and *Tipi am Kanzleramt* (Grosse Querallee, 10557, Tiergarten, www.tipi-am-kanzleramt.de).

Classical Music, Opera and Dance

The *Philharmonie* and *Kammermusiksaal* (Herbert-von-Karajan-Strasse 1, 10785, Mitte, www.berliner-philharmoniker.de) are among the most renowned concert halls in the world. The *Konzerthaus Berlin* (Gendarmenmarkt 2, 10117, Mitte, www.konzerthaus.de) presents music in a venerable setting.
The *Deutsche Oper* (Bismarckstrasse 35, 10585, Charlottenburg, www.deutscheoperberlin.de) is Berlin's largest theater; its oldest is the *Staatsoper* (Unter den Linden 7, 10117, Mitte, currently under renovation, performing until 2017 in the Schillertheater, Bismarckstrasse 100, 10585, Charlottenburg, www.staatsoper-berlin.de).

Lighter fare is performed in the *Komische Oper* (Behrenstrasse 55–57, 10117, Mitte, www. komische-oper-berlin.de) and *Neuköllner Oper* (Karl-Marx-Strasse 131–133, 12043, Neukölln, www. neukoellneroper.de). *Sasha WaltzCompany* (www.sashawaltz.de) guarantees first-class contemporary dance theater.

Event Venues
Changing exhibitions, cultural events and symposia take place at the *Academy of Arts* (Pariser Platz 4, 10117, Mitte, www.adk.de), in *Haus der Berliner Festspiele* (Schaperstrasse 24, 10719, Wilmersdorf, www. berlinerfestspiele.de), in the *House of World Cultures* (John-Foster-Dulles-Allee 10, 10557, Mitte, www.hkw.de), in *Radialsystem V* (Holzmarktstrasse 33, 10243, Friedrichshain, www.radialsystem.de) and in the *Urania* (An der Urania, 10787, Schöneberg, www.urania-berlin.de).
Popular culture events and concerts are performed at *Arena Berlin* (Eichenstrasse 4, 12435, Treptow, www. arena-berlin.de), *Columbiahalle* (Columbiadamm 13–21, 10965, Tempelhof, www.columbiahalle.de), *Estrel Berlin* (Sonnenallee 225, 12057, Neukölln, www.estrel.com), *Internationales Congress Centrum ICC* (Messedamm 11, 14055, Charlottenburg, www.icc-berlin.de), *Tempodrom* (Möckernstrasse 10, 10963, Kreuzberg, www.tempodrom. de), *Velodrom* (Paul-Heyse-Strasse 26, 10407, Pankow, www.velodrom.de) and *Arena am Ostbahnhof* (Mildred-Harnack-Strasse, 10243, Friedrichshain, www.mercedes-benz-arena.de).
Open-air concerts from opera to pop take place at the *Waldbühne* (Am Glockenturm, 14053, Charlottenburg, www.waldbuehne-berlin.de) and the *Zitadelle* (Am Juliusturm 64, 13599, Spandau, www.zitadelle-spandau.de).
Berlin's most important sports arenas are the *Arena am Ostbahnhof*, the *Max-Schmeling-Halle* (Am Falkplatz/Gaudystrasse, 10437, Pankow), the *Velodrom* and the *Olympiastadion* (Olympischer Platz, 14053, Charlottenburg).

Cinemas
In addition to the large commercial cinemas at Alexanderplatz and Potsdamer Platz, a number of traditional movie theaters still present special film programs: Theaters from the early days of film include *Babylon* (Rosa-Luxemburg-Platz 30, Mitte, www.yorck.de) and *Delphi* (Kantstrasse 12a, Charlottenburg, www.yorck.de). The movie theater in the *Hackesche Höfe* takes risks showing unconventional films (Rosenthaler Strasse 40/41, 10178, Mitte, www.hoefekino.de).
The *Astor* is one of Berlin's loveliest theaters exuding an elegant ambiance (Kurfürstendamm 225, 10719, Charlottenburg, www.astor-filmlounge.de); *International* has preserved its cheerful East German atmosphere (Karl-Marx-Allee 33, 10178, Mitte, www.yorck.de).

Museums
Current information on the most important Berlin museums and exhibitions is available at: www.smb.museum. Berlin's three central museum locations are the Museum Island (10178, Mitte), the Cultural Forum (10785, Mitte) and the Dahlem Museum Center (Lansstrasse 8, 14195, Zehlendorf). Telephone information and bookings Mon–Fri 9am–4pm at: 266 42 42 42 (service@smb. museum); on the weekend at: 266 42 30 40, 830 14 38 or 20 90 55 77. The following museums are located on *Museum Island:* Old Museum (Tue–Sun 10am–6pm, Thu until 8pm) the Old National Gallery (Tue–Sun 10am–6pm, Thu until 8pm), the Bode Museum (Tue–Sun 10am–6pm, Thu until 10pm), the New Museum (Sun–Wed 10am– 6pm, Thu–Sat 10am–8pm) and the Pergamon Museum (open daily 10am–6pm, Thu until 8pm). The *Cultural Forum* includes the Painting Gallery and the Museum of Prints and Drawings (Tue–Fri 10am–6pm, Thu until 8pm, Sat/Sun 11 am–6pm), the Museum of Decorative Arts (Tue–Fri 10am–6pm, Sat/Sun 11 am–6pm), the Musical Instrument Museum (Tue–Fri 9am–5pm, Thu until 8pm, Sat/Sun 10am–5pm) and the New National Gallery (closed for renovations until 2019). In the *Dahlem Museum Center* you'll find the Ethnological Museum, the Museum of European Cultures and the Museum of Asian Art (Tue–Fri 10am–6pm, Sat/Sun 11 am–5pm).
Other highly recommended museums are (in alphabetical order):
The *Bauhaus Archive* (Klingelhöferstrasse 14, 10785, Mitte, Wed–Mon 10am–5pm, www.bauhaus.de); the *Berggruen Museum* offering an overview of Picasso's work and life (Schlossstrasse 1, 14059, Charlottenburg, Tue–Fri 10am–6pm, Sat/Sun 11 am–6pm); the *Berlin Gallery* showing the city's local artwork from 1870 to the present (Alte Jakobstrasse 124–128, 10969, Kreuzberg, Wed–Mon 10am–6pm, www.berlinischegalerie.de);

the *Bröhan Museum* with design from the pre-Bauhaus period (Schlossstrasse 1a, 14059, Charlottenburg, Tue–Sun 10am–6pm); the *Brücke Museum* for expressionist art (Bussardsteig 9, 14195, Zehlendorf, open daily but Tuesday from 11am–5pm, www.bruecke-museum.de).
The *CharlottenburgPalace* presents the courtly lifestyle from Baroque to Classicism (Spandauer Damm 10–22, 14059, Charlottenburg, Old Palace: Tue–Sun 10am–6pm, Nov.–March until 5pm; New Wing: Wed–Mon 10am–6pm, Nov.–March until 5pm). The *Currywurst Museum* is dedicated to Berlin's culinary classic (Schützenstrasse 70, 10117, Mitte, open daily 10am–10pm, www.currywurstmuseum.de).
The *Friedrichswerder Church* is dedicated to classical architecture and sculpture (Werderscher Markt, 10117, Mitte, open daily 10am–6pm).
The *GDR Museum* presents everyday life as it existed in socialist East Germany (Karl-Liebknecht-Strasse 1, 10178, Mitte, Mon–Sun 10am–8pm, Sat 10am–10pm, www.ddr-museum.de); the *German Church* explains the German parliamentary system (Gendarmenmarkt 1, 10117, Mitte, Tue–Sun 10am–6pm, May–Sept. until 7pm); the *German Historical Museum* focuses on the country's long history (Unter den Linden 2, 10117, Mitte, open daily 10am–6pm). The *German Museum of Technology* has a large collection of technical objects (Trebbiner Strasse 9, 10963, Kreuzberg, Tue–Fri 9am–5:30pm, Sat/Sun 10am–6pm, www.technikmuseum-berlin.de); attached to it is the *Spectrum,* presenting scientific technological experiments (Möckernstrasse 26, 10963, Kreuzberg, same hours as the Museum of Technology).
The *Hamburg Station – Museum of Contemporary Art* shows Pop-Art and exhibitions of important contemporary artists (Invalidenstrasse 50/51, 10557, Mitte,Tue–Fri 10am–6pm, Thu until 8pm, Sat/Sun 11am–6pm).
The *Heinrich Zille Museum* shows drawings by the Berlin caricaturist (Propststrasse 11, 10178, Mitte, open daily 11am–6pm, April–Oct. 11am–7pm, www.heinrich-zille-museum.de). The *Huguenot Museum* recalls the French immigrants (Gendarmenmarkt 5, 10117, Mitte, Tue–Sat 12pm–5pm, Sun 11am–5pm).
The *Jewish Museum of Berlin* recounts the 2000-year history of Jewish culture in Germany (Lindenstrasse 9–14, 10969, Kreuzberg, open daily 10am–8pm, Mon 10am–10pm).
The *Käthe Kollwitz Museum* shows works by the artist (Fasanenstrasse 24, 10719, Charlottenburg, open 11am–6pm). Precious pieces of the Royal Porcelain Manufacture are displayed at *KPM Welt* (Wegelystrasse 1, 10623, Charlottenburg, Mon–Sat 10am–6pm, www.kpmberlin.de). The *Knoblauch House* focuses on the Biedermeier period (Poststraße 23, 10178, Mitte, Tue–Sun 10am–6pm, www.knoblauchhaus.de). The *Kolbe Museum* shows works by the important sculptor Georg Kolbe (Sensburger Allee 25, 14055, Charlottenburg, Tue–Sun 10am–6pm, www.georg-kolbe-museum.de).
The *Liebermann Villa* exhibits works by Max Liebermann, an artist of the Berlin Secession Movement (Colomierstrasse 3, 14109, Zehlendorf, Wed–Mon 11am–5pm, April–Sept. 10am–6pm, Thu until 8pm, www.liebermann-villa.de).
The *Märkisches Museum* is Berlin's local history museum (Am Köllnischen Park 5, 10179, Mitte, Tue–Sun 10am–6pm, www.stadtmuseum.de). The *Museum of Communication* is all about the old postal office (Leipziger Strasse 16, 10117, Mitte, Wed–Fri 9am–5pm, Tue until 8pm, Sat/Sun 10am–6pm, www.mfk-berlin.de). The *Museum of Decorative Arts* in the Köpenick Palace shows Hohenzollern treasures from Baroque to Rococo (Schlossinsel 1, 12555, Köpenick, Thu–Sun 11am–5pm). The *Museum of Film and Television* presents the movie screen heroes of the past (Potsdamer Strasse 2, 10785, Mitte, Tue–Sun 10am–6pm, Thu until 8pm). The *Museum of Natural History* shows dinosaurs, crystals and meteorites (Invalidenstrasse 43, 10115, Mitte, Tue–Fri 9:30 am–6pm, Sat/Sun 10am–6pm). The *Museum of Photography* oversees the estate of the Berlin-born photographer Helmut Newton (Jebensstrasse 2, 10623, Charlottenburg, Tue–Fri 10am–6pm, Thu until 10pm, Sat/Sun 11am–6pm, www.smb.museum).
The *Scharf-GerstenbergCollection* specializes in Surrealism (Schlossstrasse 70, 14059, Charlottenburg, Tue–Fri 10am–6pm, Sat/Sun 11am–6pm). The *St. Nicholas Church* presents medieval religious art (Nikolaikirchplatz, 10178, Mitte, open daily 10am–6pm). *The Kennedys* recalls the political clan in the United States (Pariser Platz 4a, 10117, Mitte, open daily 10am–6pm, www.thekennedys.de).

Remembrance of War, Persecution and the Division of Germany

Several memorials at historic sites commemorate the crimes committed in Germany during both 20th century dictatorships.

The era of Nazi tyranny is documented in the *House of the Wannsee Conference* (Am Grossen Wannsee 56–58, 14109, Zehlendorf, open daily 10am–6pm, www.ghwk.de); in the exhibition *"Topography of Terror"* (Niederkirchnerstrasse 8, 10963, Kreuzberg, open daily 10am–8pm) and at the *Plötzensee Memorial* (Hüttigpfad, 13627, Charlottenburg, March–Oct. open daily 9am–5pm, Nov.–Feb. 9am–4pm, www.gedenkstaette-ploetzensee.de). The *Museum of German Resistance* recalls the failed assassination attempt against Hitler in 1944 (Stauffenbergstrasse 13/14, 10785, Mitte, Mon–Fri 9am–6pm (Thu until 8pm), Sat/Sun 10am–6pm, www.gdw-berlin.de). The *German-Russian Museum* in Berlin-Karlshorst focuses on the war against Russia (Zwieseler Strasse 4, 10318, Lichtenberg, Tue–Sun 10am–6pm, www.museum-karlshorst.de).

Information on injustice and surveillance in East Germany is provided by the exhibition *"Stasi"* (Zimmerstrasse 90/91, 10117, Mitte, Mon-Sat 10am–6pm, www.bstu.bund.de); the *Stasi Museum* (former headquarters of the state security, Ruschestrasse 103, Haus 1, 10365, Lichtenberg, Mon–Fri 11am–6pm, Sat/Sun 2pm–6pm, www.stasimuseum.de) and the *Berlin-Hohenschönhausen Memorial* (former Stasi remand prison, Genslerstrasse 66, 13055, Lichtenberg, viewing only with tour, Mon–Fri 11am–3pm, Sat/Sun 10am–4pm, www.stiftung-hsh.de).

The *Allied Museum* is dedicated to the western allies (Clayallee 135, 14195, Zehlendorf, Thu–Tue 10am–6pm, www.alliiertenmuseum.de).

Information on the division of Berlin and Germany is provided at the *Berlin Wall Museum and Documentation Center* (Bernauer Strasse 111 and 119, 13355, Mitte, Tue–Sun 9:30am–6pm, April–Oct. until 7pm); the *House at Checkpoint Charlie* (Friedrichstrasse 43–45, 10969, Kreuzberg, open daily 9am–10pm); the former border crossing at the *"Palace of Tears"* (*Tränenpalast*, Reichstagufer 17, 10117, Mitte, Tue–Fri 9am–7pm, Sat/Sun 10am–6pm) and the *Marienfelde Refugee Center Museum* (Marienfelder Allee 66–80, 12277, Tempelhof, Tue–Sun 10am–6pm, www.notaufnahmelager-berlin.de).

Commemorating the Shoah is the *Memorial for the Murdered Jews of Europe*, also known as the Holocaust Memorial (Cora-Berliner-Strasse 1, 10117, Mitte, Tue–Sun 10am–8pm, Oct.–March until 7pm). The *New Guardhouse* (Unter den Linden 4, 10117, Mitte) is Germany's national memorial dedicated to all victims of war and tyranny.

NATURE

The Zoological Garden is Germany's biggest zoo with the largest collection of different species (Budapester Strasse 32 and Hardenbergplatz 8, 10787, Mitte, open daily 9am–7pm, Oct.–March 9am–5pm, www.zoo-berlin.de). The connecting aquarium is equally impressive (Budapester Strasse 32, 10787, Mitte, open daily 9am–6pm, www.aquarium-berlin.de). Tierpark Friedrichsfelde, another zoo, has expansive grounds imbedded within former palace gardens (Am Tierpark 125, 10319, Lichtenberg, open daily 9am–7pm, in winter until nightfall, www.tierpark-berlin.de).

A visit to the Botanical Gardens is a must for fans of natural vegetation from all over the world. The Tropical Greenhouse, over a 100 years old, is also impressive (Königin-Luise-Platz, 14195, Steglitz, open daily 9am until nightfall, www.botanischer-garten-berlin.de).

POLITICAL BERLIN

A visit to the Reichstag building and Reichstag cupola is only possible with an advance reservation booked through the German Bundestag Visitor Services Office (Be warned: there is a long waiting list!): Reservations can be requested by mail (Platz der Republik 1, 11011 Tiergarten), by fax 22 73 00 27 or online: www.bundestag.de. More information available by phone: Tel. 22 73 21 52.

The Federal Chancellery is open to the public during the federal government's "Open House Days" (two days in August) (Willy-Brandt-Strasse 1, 10557, Mitte, www.bundeskanzlerin.de).

The Federal Press Office runs a public information office at Dorotheenstrasse 84, 11044, Mitte (Tel. 18 27 20).

Index of sites

Index of artists and architects

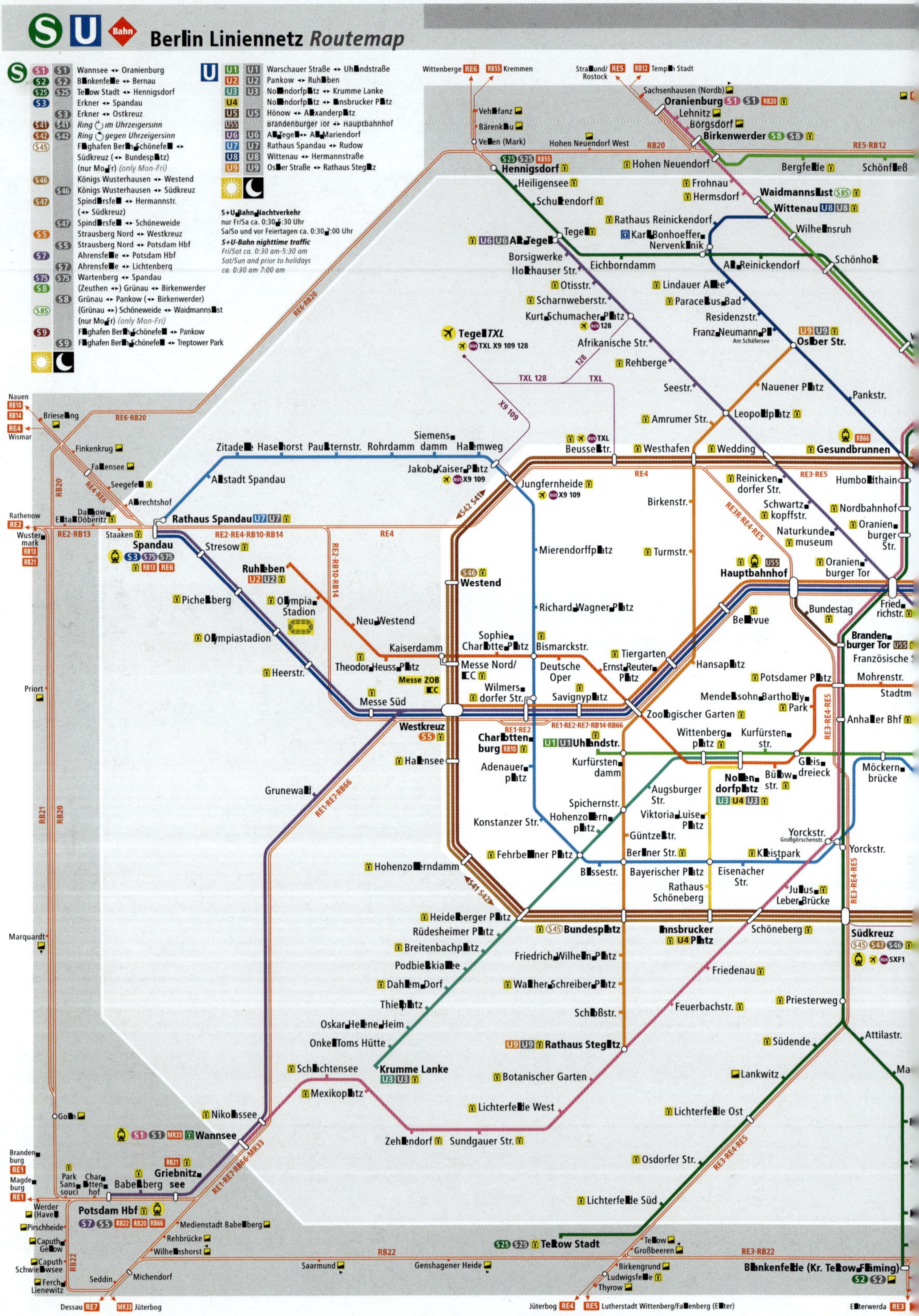

S U Bahn
Ber[redacted]in Liniennetz Routemap
S1 Wannsee ↔ Oranienburg
S2 B[redacted]ankenfe[redacted]de ↔ Bernau
S25 Te[redacted]ow Stadt ↔ Hennigsdorf
S3 Erkner ↔ Spandau
S3 Erkner ↔ Ostkreuz
S41 Ring im Uhrzeigersinn
S42 Ring gegen Uhrzeigersinn
S45 F[redacted]ughafen Ber[redacted]in-Schönefe[redacted]d ↔ Südkreuz (↔ Bundesp[redacted]atz) (nur Mo-Fr) (only Mon-Fri)
S46 Königs Wusterhausen ↔ Westend
S46 Königs Wusterhausen ↔ Südkreuz
S47 Spind[redacted]ersfe[redacted]d ↔ Hermannstr. (↔ Südkreuz)
S47 Spind[redacted]ersfe[redacted]d ↔ Schöneweide
S5 Strausberg Nord ↔ Westkreuz
S5 Strausberg Nord ↔ Potsdam Hbf
S7 Ahrensfe[redacted]de ↔ Potsdam Hbf
S7 Ahrensfe[redacted]de ↔ Lichtenberg
S75 Wartenberg ↔ Spandau
S8 (Zeuthen ↔) Grünau ↔ Birkenwerder
S8 Grünau ↔ Pankow (↔ Birkenwerder)
S85 (Grünau ↔) Schöneweide ↔ Waidmanns[redacted]ust (nur Mo-Fr) (only Mon-Fri)
S9 F[redacted]ughafen Ber[redacted]in-Schönefe[redacted]d ↔ Pankow
S9 F[redacted]ughafen Ber[redacted]in-Schönefe[redacted]d ↔ Treptower Park
U1 Warschauer Straße ↔ Uh[redacted]andstraße
U2 Pankow ↔ Ruh[redacted]eben
U3 No[redacted]endorfp[redacted]atz ↔ Krumme Lanke
U4 No[redacted]endorfp[redacted]atz ↔ [redacted]nnsbrucker P[redacted]atz
U5 Hönow ↔ A[redacted]exanderp[redacted]atz
U55 Brandenburger Tor ↔ Hauptbahnhof
U6 A[redacted]t-Tege[redacted] ↔ A[redacted]t-Mariendorf
U7 Rathaus Spandau ↔ Rudow
U8 Wittenau ↔ Hermannstraße
U9 Os[redacted]oer Straße ↔ Rathaus Steg[redacted]itz
S+U-Bahn-Nachtverkehr
nur Fr/Sa ca. 0:30-5:30 Uhr
Sa/So und vor Feiertagen ca. 0:30-7:00 Uhr
S+U-Bahn nighttime traffic
Fri/Sat ca. 0:30 am-5:30 am
Sat/Sun and prior to holidays ca. 0:30 am-7:00 am